ROLAND SMITH

With photographs by JOHN CLEARE

ON FOOT IN THE YORKSHIRE DALES

35 Circular Routes from the Nidd to the Swale

DAVID & CHARLES

Maps by MARK RICHARDS

A DAVID & CHARLES BOOK

First published in the UK in 1996
Copyright © Roland Smith 1996
Copyright © photographs: John Cleare 1996

Roland Smith has asserted his right to be identified as author of this work in accordance with the Copyright, Designs and Patents Act 1988.

A catalogue record for this book is available from the British Library.

ISBN 0 7153 0366 X

Typeset by ABM Typographics Ltd, Hull
and printed in Italy by Milanostampa SpA
for David & Charles
Brunel House   Newton Abbot   Devon

Cover photographs: (front) The author on the summit of The Nab, Wild Boar Fell, looking across Mallerstang (see Walk 23); (back) On the Dales Way, near Barden Bridge, looking north-west towards Club Nook
Page 1: Herb Robert and hart's-tongue fern growing among the grikes of a limestone pavement

To the memory of Dr Arthur Raistrick, (1897–1991), geologist, historian, industrial archaeologist, author, conservationist and rambler – the greatest Dalesman of his age.

Acknowledgements: Any honest author writing in the Dales must acknowledge their debt to the scholars of the past, and I am no exception. This book is dedicated to the greatest of them all, Arthur Raistrick, but it also owes much to the works of Alfred Brown, Ella Pontefract, Marie Hartley and Joan Ingilby. Many of the walks were suggested to me by the excellent Hillside Publications of my good friend, Paul Hannon.

Finally, I must again pay tribute to the patient and loving forebearance of my wife, Val, and our family.

By the same author
On Foot in the Pennines
First and Last
Wildest Britain
Peak National Park (official guide)
Walking the Great Views
Explore Britain's National Parks

INTRODUCTION: DALES IN PARADISE   **4**
EXPLANATORY NOTES   **11**

1 WHARFEDALE: QUEEN OF THEDALES   **13**
Walk 1 The Strid and Simon's Seat   16
Walk 2 The Gill of the Trolls   19
Walk 3 The Limestone Wonders of Wharfedale   21
Walk 4 Hebden's Leaden Legacy   24
Walk 5 The Ascent of Buckden Pike   26
Walk 6 Great Whernside – Monarch
     of Wharfedale   28

**2 NIDDERDALE: DALE OF LOST
   OPPORTUNITY**   **31**
Walk 7 The Work of Druids?   34
Walk 8 Around the Upper Nidd   36
Walk 9 Fountains Abbey and Studley Royal   39

**3 MALHAMDALE: SCAR, TARN
   AND GORGE**   **43**
Walk 10 A Malham Meander   46
Walk 11 Pikedaw and Nappa Cross   47
Walk 12 Gothic Gordale and Monastic Mastiles   49
Walk 13 Airton and Kirkby Malham   52

4 RIBBLESDALE: THREE PEAKS COUNTRY   **55**
Walk 14 'Hill of the Winds'   58
Walk 15 The Caves of Attermire   60
Walk 16 The Waterfalls Walk   63

CONTENTS

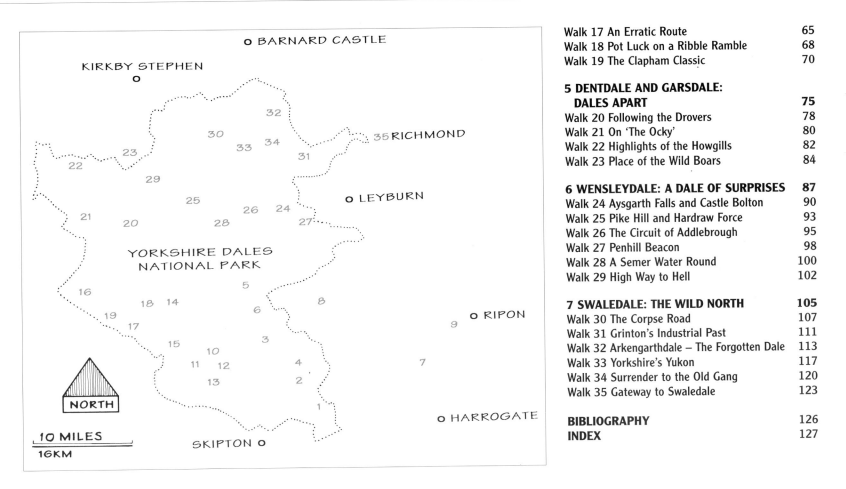

BARNARD CASTLE

KIRKBY STEPHEN

32

30
33 34
23
22
35 RICHMOND
31

29

LEYBURN

25
26 24
21
20 28 27

YORKSHIRE DALES
NATIONAL PARK

5

16
18 14 8
6
19
17 9 RIPON

15
10
11 12 4
13 2 7

NORTH

1

10 MILES
16KM HARROGATE

SKIPTON

Walk 17 An Erratic Route   65
Walk 18 Pot Luck on a Ribble Ramble   68
Walk 19 The Clapham Classic   70

**5 DENTDALE AND GARSDALE:
    DALES APART   75**
Walk 20 Following the Drovers   78
Walk 21 On 'The Ocky'   80
Walk 22 Highlights of the Howgills   82
Walk 23 Place of the Wild Boars   84

6 WENSLEYDALE: A DALE OF SURPRISES   87
Walk 24 Aysgarth Falls and Castle Bolton   90
Walk 25 Pike Hill and Hardraw Force   93
Walk 26 The Circuit of Addlebrough   95
Walk 27 Penhill Beacon   98
Walk 28 A Semer Water Round   100
Walk 29 High Way to Hell   102

7 SWALEDALE: THE WILD NORTH   105
Walk 30 The Corpse Road   107
Walk 31 Grinton's Industrial Past   111
Walk 32 Arkengarthdale – The Forgotten Dale   113
Walk 33 Yorkshire's Yukon   117
Walk 34 Surrender to the Old Gang   120
Walk 35 Gateway to Swaledale   123

BIBLIOGRAPHY   126
INDEX   127

INTRODUCTION: DALES IN PARADISE

There must be dales in Paradise,
Which you and I will find,
And walk together dalesmen-wise,
And smile (since God is kind)
At all the foreign peoples there
Enchanted by our blessed air!

That incorrigible fellwanderer Alfred J. Brown's indignant outburst to 'Pater' in *Four Boon Fellows* (1928), gives some indication of the unswerving loyalty felt by true dalesmen to their homeland. The thought that Heaven could exist *without* that intoxicating mixture of dale and moor, waterfall and woodland which makes up the incomparable Yorkshire Dales was to him, quite simply inconceivable.

Four Boon Fellows – the title refers to the four major rivers which drain the Dales, the Wharfe, Aire, Ouse and Swale – is actually a stinging diatribe against what Brown disparagingly refers to as the 'Hogs' who were taking over his beloved land.

'…this little land of ours is beset by a hideous invader; a ubiquitous Thing on Wheels of multiple forms, but of one devouring purpose, which is to eat up our very roads, to tear up our very byways, to massacre our few remaining Shanks's Mares, to choke the last Guard of the old legion of Walkers, to throw dust in their eyes, to set traps for their legs, and, in a word, to knock them down and exterminate them utterly.'

And those 'rushing and roaring…stinking and shrieking' Things on Wheels were piloted by 'Hogs', identified by 'a pair of oily hands (for oil is of the very essence of the Things), a pair of woebegone and – preferably – begoggled eyes and (of course) a Roaring Horn to tear, chew and gollop as many miles as are left between Land's End and John o'Groats'.

Although written nearly seventy years ago, Brown's bitter harangue against the motorcar could (minus the goggles, perhaps) be echoed today, especially on a busy Bank Holiday Monday on the roads approaching Grassington, Hawes or Malham.

This book is most definitely **not** aimed at the Hogs, nor their two-wheeled compatriots whom Brown dubbed the Hoggets. Rather it is directed at what Brown called 'the Last of the Walkers', whom he gloomily considered would soon be following the Last of the Vikings into the dim renown of legend.

But Brown was being unduly pessimistic about the demise of walkers – the hobby has never been more popular. And with over 1100 miles (1770km) of public rights-of-way and some of the country's finest limestone and grit-stone scenery, the 683sq mile (1769 sq km) Yorkshire Dales National Park is Britain's third largest after the Lake District and Snowdonia.

Most of the nine million annual visits to the Dales National Park are still made by car, of course, but many of today's 'Hogs' seem prepared to leave their metal boxes behind for at least part of their visit, and so become properly acquainted with what another loyal Yorkshireman, J. B. Priestley, called the 'entrancing variety' of the Dales.

Man-made Landscape

There are few scenes more instantly identifiable as English than a typical view of one of the northern dales from the moorland heights above. I have in mind the view of Muker in Swaledale from the old bridleway above Gun Ing Lane. The compact grey village, dominated by the tower of its medieval church, seems to grow almost organically from the native rock. It sits like a spider at the centre of an intricate web of drystone walls spreading up the slopes of Kisdon above, and every couple of enclosed meadows seem to have their own little gabled barn ready to take the summer's harvest of sweet-smelling, herb-rich hay.

In the valley bottom, where the swirling Swale is joined by the Straw Beck, clumps of

The gorge of the Swale from Crackpot Hall

4

trees soften the scene. But above on the fellsides, the native limestone breaks through to the surface in the 'scars' of Thwaite Stones and Kisdon Scar. And in the background, there is always the constant backdrop of the brooding moors, leading up to the lonely, evocatively named summits of Lovely Seat and Shunner Fell.

This idyllic scene is repeated in the upper reaches of most of the dales and it represents a perfect picture of the way in which Man has harmoniously shaped the Dales landscape over the past 8,000 years. It also emphasises the fact that the Dales landscape, which was the prime reason for it being designated a National Park in 1954, is essentially man-made, created by the patient stewardship of generations of dales people.

This was recognised in the Yorkshire Dales National Park's 'Landscapes for Tomorrow' project, an experiment in interpreting the landscapes of the future, specifically aimed at the local population. It asked people what sort of landscape they preferred, and the choices ranged from an abandoned wilderness to an intensively farmed or a leisure-based landscape. Not surprisingly, most people said that the features they most enjoyed were the traditional ones of drystone walls and field barns, woodlands, moorlands and hay meadows – exactly the kind of scene described above near Muker.

Left: A beautiful herb-rich flower meadow at Starbotton, Wharfedale
Opposite: Karst country – limestone pavements near Sulber Nick, Ribblesdale

But in today's world, that landscape no longer just happens automatically, and the landscape which most people preferred was described as 'conserved', that is, created and sustained by public money made available to farmers to farm in an environmentally sensitive way, encouraging heather moorland, flower-rich meadows, field barns and broad-leaved woodland.

In 1986 this fact was further recognised by the designation of the Pennine Dales Environmentally Sensitive Area. This has since been extended to cover most of the northern dales of Wharfedale with Littondale, Langstrothdale, Dentdale with Deepdale, and Swaledale with Arkengarthdale – a total of fifteen per cent of the area of the National Park. Under the ESA scheme, farmers receive payments for conservation-based farming, and this has since been augmented by the National Park's own Barns and Walls Conservation Scheme in Swaledale and Arkengarthdale. All this makes the point that even the most natural-looking landscapes still need to be sensitively managed and conserved.

The Roots of Scenery

Before Man arrived on the scene, the Yorkshire Dales was a virgin landscape shaped by countless aeons of deposition, folding, faulting and erosion and finally polished by the tremendous grinding power of the Ice Age glaciers, which were the architects of the dales themselves.

The bedrock of the Yorkshire Dales constitute some of the earliest formations known to Man. The delicately pastel-shaded Ordovician slates exposed under the waterfalls of the Ingleton Glens have been estimated at about 500 million years old, and the celebrated 'unconformity' shown at Thornton Force is one of Britain's classic geological sites.

Here upstanding, jagged-edged Ordovician slates are directly overlaid by a solid horizontal bed of Carboniferous limestone. The geological time gap between the two formations is an unimaginable 200 to 400 million years, or as much time as has elapsed between when the limestone was laid down and today.

I'll never forget a lecture in which the great Dales academic, Arthur Raistrick, described this as 'almost a terrifying geological feature, if you think too much about it'. And he added: 'I have never been up there without standing and putting my hand on the junction between the two types of rock and trying to think just what it means'. Try it and you'll see just what a mind-blowing experience it can be.

The next oldest rocks are the Silurian slates which make up the seductively smooth-sided Howgill Fells near Sedburgh in the north-west corner of the National Park. These are 440 million years old, and both geologically and physically much more closely aligned to the Lake District hills across the M6.

More than ninety per cent of the Yorkshire Dales National Park is made up of Carboniferous rocks, laid down under semi-tropical conditions over 300 million years ago, at a time when what we now know as Britain was much closer to the Equator.

That's a hard concept for the modern walker to appreciate as he or she battles across Mastiles Moor or the limestone pavements of Ingleborough into the teeth of a mad March gale throwing stinging handfuls of sleet or snow into their face. But if they look more closely at the limestone beneath their feet, they may just come across the skeletal remains of the long-dead sea creatures whose fossilised bodies created the rock.

The Yorkshire Dales represent one of the finest glacio-karst (limestone affected by glaciers) landscapes in Britain. The central block of limestone, known as the Great Scar or Craven Limestone, stretches between Wharfedale in the east to beyond Ingleborough in the west and is about 800ft (244m) deep.

This is the landscape for which the Dales are best known and this is the landscape, in W. H. Auden's celebrated poem *In Praise of Limestone*, which makes the expatriot dalesman most homesick.

…Mark these rounded slopes with their surface
   fragrance of thyme and, beneath,
A secret system of caves and conduits: hear the
   springs
That spurt out everywhere with a chuckle,
Each filling a private pool for fish and carving
Its own little ravine whose cliffs entertain
The butterfly and the lizard:

It is in this massively bedded rock that the great scenic wonders of the Dales are found, such as the breathtaking 260ft (80m) high amphitheatre of Malham Cove, the awe-inspiring gorge

of Gordale Scar and the brooding overhang of Kilnsey Crag. They were carved by the awesome power of Ice Age glaciers or their meltwaters. The tremendous natural planing effect of those same glaciers shaved off the surface soil to expose the so-called limestone pavements, with their intricate jigsaw of clints and grikes, so well seen above Malham Cove, on Moughton and on Southerscales Scar below Ingleborough.

No rambler competent with a compass should ever get lost on an area of limestone pavement – although there is always the risk of a broken or twisted ankle for the careless. For as Arthur Raistrick again pointed out, all the major joints, or grikes, run about fifteen degrees west of north in limestone pavements throughout the northern hemisphere.

It is within the shady and damp recesses of the grikes of limestone pavements that some of the most beautiful botanic treasures of the Dales can be found. Here in these sheltered, greenhouse conditions, lime-loving plants such as hart's-tongue fern, the vivid scarlet bloody cranesbill and the white bells of lily of the valley flourish, safe from the nibbling teeth of sheep and the withering effects of the wind.

The other, often unseen, features of limestone are Auden's 'secret systems' of pot-holes and caves which have been formed by underground streams and the slightly acidic effect of rainwater. The most famous of these are open to the public, such as the Ingleborough and White Scar Caves near Ingleton, and Stump Cross Cavern near Pateley Bridge.

Other true pot-holes such as the huge maw of Gaping Gill (the biggest in Britain) and Alum Pot on the slopes of Ingleborough and Hull Pot below Pen-y-Ghent, are so-called 'sporting' caves and strictly the preserve of properly equipped troglodytes – well beyond the experience of the sun- and sky-loving pedestrian who is the object of this book.

Many of the highest hills in the Yorkshire Dales, such as Ingleborough, Pen-y-Ghent, Penhill and Addlebrough, have a distinctive stepped profile which adds a certain air of nobility to their appearance. It comes as no surprise to learn that as late as the early nineteenth century, the Craven hills were still thought to be the highest in England.

The reason for this is that the later Carboniferous rocks of the Dales were laid down in a sequence which is known as the Yoredale series, which takes its name from the old name for the River Ure. The uppermost strata of this Yoredale series is the dark, abrasive sandstone known as millstone grit, and in the case of the highest peaks this often forms a resistant cap over the earlier shales and limestone deposits. It was formed as sandbanks and deltas laid down by huge Amazonian rivers flowing from the north in the later Carboniferous period.

Millstone grit also predominates in the larger, poorly drained areas of moorland above the dales themselves, where rank moor grass and the fluffy white heads of cotton grass – locally and appropriately known as 'bog-baby-warning' – are among the few plants which can exist on the deep, soggy peat. Heather moorland, where the red grouse is king, is generally found in slightly drier areas, such as Barden Fell and Moor in Wharfedale.

The Coming of Man

It is easy to describe these open, windswept moors as the 'wilderness' areas of the Yorkshire Dales. But, as we will see, even these apparently wild landscapes have all been affected in one way or another by Man's activities, and only deeply cut becks or crag faces have escaped his all-pervading influence.

The discovery of minute flint chippings on the highest moors shows that as early as Mesolithic times (up to 10,000 years ago) these inhospitable areas were being used by summer hunting parties, and the great clearance of the native wildwood (for apart from the very highest summits, even today's moorland was then wooded) had begun.

These earliest settlers left little to mark their passing, apart from their discarded flint weapons. The only substantial evidence of Stone Age man has been in some of the more accessible caves where they sheltered while waiting for passing game, such as Victoria Cave, east of Settle, or Foxholes in Clapdale, above Clapham.

Elsewhere, only the enigmatic 'stone circle' at Yockenthwaite, in Langstrothdale (which is much more likely to be the remains of the enclosing kerb of a burial mound), and the Castle Dykes henge near Aysgarth, standing

A showery day at Norber above Austwick in Ribblesdale

high on a shoulder between Bishopdale and Wensleydale, give any clues to their lifestyle.

It was during the Bronze and Iron Ages that the frontiers of farming were really pushed forward, and the legend 'Celtic Fields', still shown on maps especially around Grassington, Malham or at Carpley Green and around the flanks of Addlebrough, show just how intensive that agriculture was. Still visible in aerial photographs or under the right lighting conditions are the fields, huts, cattle pounds, burial mounds and roadways of what must have been a large population of the people who became the first true dalesmen.

Easily the most visible and impressive monument from the Iron Age is the magnificent hill fort of Ingleborough, which encircles the 2372ft (723m) summit and is the highest in England. The pear-shaped, 15 acre (6ha) enclosure contains the remains of a large number of hut

A typical Dales field barn near Skyreholme in Wharfedale

circles, showing that in the summer months at least, a sizeable population lived within its massive stone walls. Like most hill forts, it was probably more often used as a summer 'shieling' than a defensive site, despite the persistent legend of Venutious of the Brigantes and his last stand against the invading Romans. It is still a magnificent viewpoint and the goal of every true-born hill-walking Yorkshireman.

The coming of the Romans established the classic dual economy of the Dales which was to last for the next millenium and beyond. The riches of wool, hides and meat from the already extensive grazing grounds of the dales was now to be supplemented for the first time by the exploitation of the mineral wealth of the hills, in particular, lead.

Pigs of lead dating from the reigns of Trajan and Hadrian have been discovered in the Dales, as the legions slowly but surely infiltrated the hills from their regional headquarters at York (Eboracum). But the next wave of invaders, the Saxons and the Vikings, were to leave a much more lasting legacy.

You can trace the spread of these barbarian hordes by studying the place-names on a map of the Dales. To the east of the Dales, there is a distinct Danish influence in place-names, typically ending with 'by'. But west of this and in the lower parts of the dales, village names ending in 'ley' indicate a forest clearing made by Anglians from the Low Countries around the Baltic.

West of this in the bleak, higher reaches of the Dales, the influence of the Norsemen who reached the Dales from Scotland and Ireland between the ninth and eleventh centuries is everywhere. Words like 'clint', 'beck' and 'foss' are all pure Norse and sure indicators that these high sheep pastures were first settled by Vikings and Norsemen, who felt more at home in these isolated communities and empty fellsides. They also bred the archetypal Dalesmen; stern, independent free-thinkers who prefer to keep themselves to themselves.

The Norman invasion saw William's 'harrying of the north', a chilling and deliberate depopulation pogrom almost unparalleled in Europe until Hitler's holocaust. This systematic clearance of the troublesome peasantry was supervised from forbidding castles like Skipton, Middleham and Richmond. During the Middle Ages another, more peaceful influence swept through the Dales in the form of vast sheep ranches supervised by 'granges' and run by the land-hungry monks of the great religious houses like Fountains Abbey in Skelldale and Jervaulx in Wensleydale. The white-robed monks who gloried in their poverty were, paradoxically, also great entrepreneurs and among the first to build mills to harness the water power of Dales rivers.

Thankfully, water-powered industrialisation, which so drastically altered the lower reaches of the rivers during the eighteenth and nineteenth centuries, largely passed the Dales by. One industry, however, left lasting scars, especially in places like Swaledale and its subsidiary valleys, and it was the one initiated by the Romans – lead. Its modern counterpart – limestone extraction – threatens to do even more lasting and large-scale damage to the precious Dales landscape.

Despite all the changes through this long and varied history, today's visitor to the Yorkshire Dales sees a settled and largely peaceful landscape. 'It is,' insisted Alfred Brown, 'a landscape which brings those prepared to explore it on foot as close to Heaven as you can get on Earth.' Without more ado, let us follow his invitation:

There must be dales in Paradise
With noble tops atween:
Swart fells uprearing to the skies
And stretching to the green
And 'ower t'tops' we two shall go,
Knee-deep in ling and broom or snow!

EXPLANATORY NOTES

One of the great joys of the Yorkshire Dales is that each dale is different and has its own individual character. From the soft, sylvan reaches of Wensleydale and Dentdale to the stern northern wilderness of Swaledale, each has its personal story to tell.

The Walks

This book looks at each of the seven major dales in turn, starting with a brief general description of its natural and human history including most points of interest available to the walker.

This is followed by a selection of some of the best and most typical walks in each dale, exploring some of those special landscapes which can only be reached on foot. Most walks are fairly short and circular, enabling the walker to return to his or her transport. The responsible walker in a pressurised area like the Yorkshire Dales should use public transport wherever possible, and some of the finest walking in the National Park can be reached by the spectacular Settle–Carlisle railway. This also provides the walker with the opportunity for linear routes, returning to your starting point by this most monumental rail line.

A Fact File and route summary at the end of each walk gives an at-a-glance précis of the route and its difficulty. Note that where the left or right bank of a beck is mentioned, it is as the walker sees it – i.e. it is not the **true** left or right as the stream descends.

Equipment

Walkers leaving the valley routes in the Dales for the higher tops should be properly equipped with warm, wind and waterproof clothing and boots or strong walking shoes. Although none of the summits top 3000ft (914m), they should never be under-estimated in view of their extreme northern latitude.

The other essential for walking on the tops is a compass and the knowledge of how to use it. Mist and rain can descend with frightening rapidity in the Yorkshire Dales, and places like Ingleborough or the Howgills can be deceptive and dangerous.

Maps

The sketch maps which accompany each walk are included purely to give an indication of the walk location. To undertake any of the walks described in this book, you should also use the appropriate Ordnance Survey map.

The Dales walker is fortunate that most of the National Park is covered by the OS's excellent Outdoor Leisure 1:25 000, 2½in to 1 mile (4cm to 1km) series. The appropriate maps are: OL2, Yorkshire Dales Western Area (covering the Three Peaks country of Whernside, Ingleborough and Pen-y-Ghent); OL10, Yorkshire Dales Southern Area (covering Malham and Central Wharfedale); OL30, Yorkshire Dales Northern and Central Areas (covering Wensleydale, Swaledale and Upper Nidderdale), and OL19, the Howgill Fells and Upper Eden Valley. Lower Nidderdale is covered by Pathfinders 630 (SE 17/18) Middleham and Jervaulx Abbey; 652 (SE 16) Pateley Bridge; and 653 (SE 26/36) Fountains Abbey and Boroughbridge.

There is also the 1:63 360 (1in to 1 mile) Ordnance Survey Touring Map and Guide to the Yorkshire Dales, which covers the whole of the National Park. This is useful for general location work but not so good for walking, as field boundaries are not shown.

Long-distance Paths

Several official and unofficial long-distance paths thread the Yorkshire Dales, the most famous of which is Tom Stephenson's marathon, the Pennine Way. Britain's toughest and most pressurised National Trail runs for about 60 miles (96.5km) through the Yorkshire Dales, crossing the grain of the country between Gargrave and Tan Hill. Where it coincides with the Dales famous one-day marathon, the Three Peaks Walk, especially over Pen-y-Ghent, it has been subject to the most horrific erosion and generally should be avoided by seekers of solitude. The 84 mile (135km) Dales Way is an easier Dales classic, linking the Dales with the Lake District from Ilkley to Windermere using mainly riverside paths through Wharfedale and Dentdale. The Ribble Way's northern extremity follows that river from Settle through to its source at Ribblehead, while Wainwright's Coast-to-Coast route crosses the watershed at the head of Swaledale, and follows it through to Richmond.

WHARFEDALE:
QUEEN OF THE DALES

Beautiful Wharfedale, so sweet and so fair,
Nowhere in England can with thee compare.

This old song of Wharfedale by Willie Foster of Beckermonds was regularly performed at a special ceremony on New Year's Day in the George Inn, Hubberholme. The occasion was the annual 'land letting' of the tenancy of the Poor Pasture – a meadow behind the inn which, like the pub itself, was owned by the Church Commissioners.

The old custom was recalled by Ella Pontefract and Marie Hartley in *Wharfedale*, their charming evocation of the dale as it was in the late 1930s. Their description of Wharfedale as 'a valley favoured by nature and enriched by romance' can hardly be improved today, and it is many people's favourite dale.

That ancient land-letting ceremony at Hubberholme says much about the history of the dale. There had been yeoman farmers named Foster at Beckermonds, the isolated hamlet where the Green Field Beck meets the

Wharfe, since the seventeenth century. In 1765 we read that a Magret Foster [sic] was paid 2d for her 'Trouble' in assisting at the funeral of Margret Parker.

The place names tell us much about the earliest settlers in the upper reaches of Wharfedale, the first people who made their homes among the bleak hills of Langstrothdale's.

Langstrothdale Chase – an ancient hunting forest administered from Barden Tower, the hunting tower of the Cliffords further down the dale – is the name commonly given to the upper reaches of Wharfedale. The river rises as Oughtershaw Beck on the very watershed of England at Cam Houses, where a bunkhouse barn now provides basic accommodation for walkers on the Dales Way.

Beckermonds is a pure Old Norse name meaning junction of the streams, while Hubberholme seems to mean 'Hunburg's home', or 'piece of land surrounded by streams', from the Old Scandinavian tongue. Other Norse names in the higher reaches of the dale, such as Yockenthwaite ('Eogan's clearing') and Starbotton ('inner valley where

stakes were obtained') also show how Norsemen coming across the hills from Ireland and the Lake District found this wilder part of the dale to their liking.

The connection with the church is also significant, for much of Wharfedale's history of landownership is closely tied to ecclesiastical affairs. The great estates of the monks of Bolton Abbey (or more accurately, Priory) at the foot of the dale, and Fountains Abbey in nearby Nidderdale, spread well into Wharfedale, largely creating today's sheep pastures.

The influence of Fountains is especially felt around the great overhanging cowl of Kilnsey Crag, where the seventeenth-century Kilnsey Old Hall was built on the site of the medieval grange of the Cistercians. One of the great walking experiences of the Dales is to follow in the sandal-clad footsteps of the white-robed monks along the walled green drover's road of Mastiles Lane, which linked their Kilnsey and Malham estates.

Kilnsey Crag is the geomorphological show-place of Wharfedale, marking precisely the height of the Ice Age glacier which cleanly sliced off the spur of limestone which projected into

A field barn in Langstrothdale

the millstone grit moorland giants of Great Whernside (2308ft/704m) and Buckden Pike (2302ft/702m) now left behind but both providing the walker with superb viewpoints of the upper reaches of the dale.

The busy little village of Grassington is in many respects the capital of Wharfedale. Although its quaint cobbles and teeming crowds of summer visitors sometimes give it a West Country air, historically its wealth and very existence was founded on industry – and that industry was lead.

The remains of 't'owd man', as the ancient lead miners are known, are evident everywhere in the green hillsides around Grassington, especially in the area of Grassington Moor around Yarnbury, where the moor is covered with spoil heaps and potentially dangerous disused mines and shafts. During the heyday of the lead mining industry (1790–1860), Grassington was the centre of one of the most flourishing lead mining areas in the whole of Yorkshire.

Lower down the daleside, north of Grassington in the area of Lea Green, there are extensive remains of field systems, clearance cairns, settlements and deserted villages which

the valley. During the Ice Ages, powerful glaciers swept down both Wharfedale and Littondale, the valley of the River Skirfare. As they retreated about 15,000 years ago, they left a moraine dam at Mill Scar Lash, flooding the valley with an enormous lake, which accounts for the unusual flatness of the valley floor between Kilnsey and Conistone.

Kilnsey also marks the limit of the white-walled limestone country of Wharfedale, with

indicate just how extensively the area was settled in Romano-British and even earlier times.

The area around Thorpe and Appletreewick is characterised by small, conical hills such as Butter Haw, Kail and Elbolton, which are the remains of harder reef limestone knolls formed on the edge of coral reefs in the Carboniferous sea.

Below Grassington, Burnsall and Appletreewick, the Wharfe twists between the moorland bastions of Barden Fell and Moor, where the four-square ruins of the Clifford's Barden Tower occupy a strategic position near Barden Bridge.

We are back in millstone grit country again now, as the dark heather moorlands around Simon's Seat (1591ft/485m) and Bardon Moor indicate. Here, agreements between the National Park authority and the Duke of Devonshire give free access for the walker to explore the tors and crags of the higher moors and some of the finest views of Wharfedale.

In the now thickly wooded valley below, the Wharfe is forced into the famous constriction known as The Strid, a short walk upstream from the popular honeypot of the Duke's estate of Bolton Abbey, a favourite weekend resort for the residents of the industrial towns and cities of the West Riding. The partly ruined Augustinian priory with its gaping eastern arch is a fine example of Early English architecture, built at a time when the canons still ruled the dale.

Perhaps it was the easy accessibility of Wharfedale, and Bolton Abbey in particular, which attracted writers and artists like no other dale in Yorkshire. Ever since the days of William Camden, who called the Wharfe 'forward, stubborn and angry', through to Thomas Pennant, William Wordsworth, J. M. W. Turner and Alfred Lord Tennyson, Wharfedale has excited romantics. But perhaps its finest description comes from John Ruskin, who made his first visit to the Dales in 1862 while working on his *Modern Painters*, and frequently visited Bolton Abbey.

Noble moorlands extend above, purple with heath, and broken into scars and glens; and around every soft tuft of wood, and gentle extent of meadow, throughout the dale, there floats a feeling of this mountain power, and an instinctive apprehension of the strength and greatness of the wild northern land.

THE STRID AND SIMON'S SEAT

The elegant, romantic ruins of Bolton Abbey (actually a priory) command the entrance to Wharfedale. They are a justly popular weekend destination for the people of the teeming cities of the West Riding, especially on summer weekends. But for every discerning walker who heads away from the crowds at the famous Stepping Stones towards the commanding viewpoints of Simon's Seat, Barden Fell and Lord's Seat, there will be twenty who do not stray from the wooded surrounds of the Augustinian Priory, which is a good enough recommendation for me.

Follow the signs for the Dales Way from the Cavendish Pavilion (refreshments) off the B6160 north of the abbey. Walk upstream on the western bank for about a mile (1.6km) through the trees of Strid Wood to reach the roaring cataract of The Strid (1). Massive gritstone buttresses squeeze the river into a narrow 6½ft (2m) wide channel, like a small-scale version of High Force. It was here in Scott's epic poem that the Boy of Egremond, son of Alice de Romily of Skipton Castle, was drowned attempting to leap the chasm while on a deer hunt. He was the first, but not the last, to be drowned here, so take special care.

Return to the Dales Way and cross the river by a classical-looking footbridge, which is actually an aquaduct (2), turning right returning down the riverside path, passing The Strid again on your right now, through Park Plantation to join the minor road near Posforth Bridge.

Turn sharp left to a gate on the left with an open access notice. These moors are subject to an access agreement between the Devonshire estate and the Yorkshire Dales National Park. Through the gate, the sandy track winds up above wooded Posforth Gill (3). Through the trees, the gill tumbles down the lace-like Posforth Falls and a lovely waterslide, which are well-worth a detour if you have the time.

Cross a footbridge to enter the Valley of Desolation, named after a seventeenth-century precursor of the 1987 hurricane, which devastated the trees of Laund Pasture Plantation. The track enters the plantation and then emerges on the open heather grouse moor at Great Agill Bottom.

Cross Great Agill Beck by a ford, then climb steeply to a stone table where another shooter's track leads off to the right. Keep left here (4), following the path through the heather, eventually crossing the headwaters of the beck and climbing up to the rocks of Truckle Crags.

The tors of Hen Stones are over to the right.

The summit crags of Simon's Seat (1591ft/ 485m) now beckon on the skyline ahead, and an enjoyable little rocky scramble takes you to the highest point of the massive gritstone tors which mark the summit. From the white trig point, the view north takes in the length of Wharfedale, with the conical reef-limestone knolls around Appletreewick and Skyreholme and the deep ravine of Trollers Gill prominent in front. To the south, the view extends to Pendle Hill, with Fountains Fell, Buckden Pike and Great Whernside visible to the north-west.

After drinking in this superb viewpoint, head eastwards (5) to the only slightly inferior summit tors of Lord's Seat, (1565ft/477m). From Lord's Seat, follow the drystone wall to the right which leads past a series of grouse butts to the shooter's track which you passed on your way up. This descends easily through the heather beneath the tors of Hen Stones, above and to your right. After about half a mile, you regain your outward path by the stone table just below Great Agill Head.

Now it is a simple matter of retracing your steps (6) back down through the Valley of Desolation and Launds Pasture Plantation, to your car and the waiting welcome refreshments available at the Cavendish Pavilion.

Just upstream from the Strid, a heron waits patiently by the Wharfe for a passing meal

Map OS Outdoor Leisure Sheet 10, Yorkshire Dales (Southern Area)
Start/Finish Cavendish Pavilion, Bolton Abbey GR 077552
Length About 9 miles (14.5km)
Walking time Allow 4–5 hours
Difficulty Easy woodland and moorland tracks to a rocky summit

The Route in Brief

Start GR 077552, from the car park at the Cavendish Pavilion off the B6160.
1 Follow the Dales Way from the Wooden Bridge upstream (N) on the W bank of the River Wharfe for about 1 mile (1.6km) to inspect The Strid.
2 Continue upstream through the woods to an aquaduct. Cross the river and turn R downstream back to the minor road at Posforth Bridge.
3 Turn sharp L following Posforth Gill and into the Valley of Desolation.
4 Through Laund Pasture Plantation, turn L
following Great Agill Beck towards Truckle Crags.
5 Ascend the summit rocks of Simon's Seat then head E to Lord's Seat, following wall R around Hen
Stones and back to Great Agill Bottom.
6 Retrace your steps through the Valley of Desolation and back to the Cavendish Pavilion.

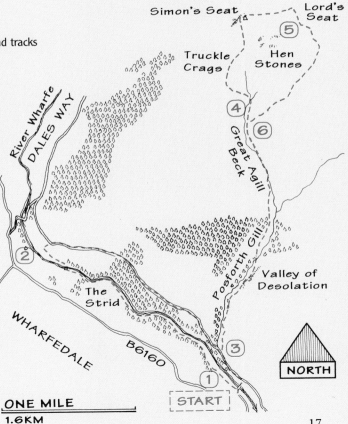

17

THE GILL OF THE TROLLS

Trollers Gill is a place of mystery and folklore, a miniature Gordale Scar tucked away above the Wharfe and beneath Simon's Seat. It takes its name from trolls or fairies who were apparently adept at rolling stones down hillsides in the dead of night. It is also said to be the home of a 'barghest' – a spectral dog the size of a bear with eyes like saucers which, if they met yours, could mean instant death. Trollers Gill is just one highlight of this beautiful walk around the interesting limestone country of mid-Wharfedale. It features a superb length of the Dales Way alongside the Wharfe south from the attractive village of Burnsall.

Burnsall is one of the loveliest villages in Wharfedale, standing at the junction where the gritstone gives way to the limestone. The Old Grammar School and the mainly fifteenth-century church of St Wilfred's, which has some interesting earlier remains, are highlights, and I particularly like the name of the beck which runs off Burnsall Fell to join the Wharfe in the village, known as Joy Beck, after a local family.

Our walk starts from the large riverside car park. Cross the bridge over the Wharfe, turning right down to the eastern bank where a signpost indicates Howgill. This is the Dales Way, which we follow for the next couple of miles alongside the babbling Wharfe (**1**).

Crossing a footbridge by Woodhouse Farm, the route passes close by the river in a narrow, wooded gorge beneath conical Kail Hill, a reef limestone peak and one of two 'Kail Hills' on either side of the river near Burnsall. Passing a caravan site and Appletreewick up to the left, the way keeps faithfully to the river bank until it climbs up to the lane at the hamlet of Howgill.

Turn left here then right (**2**) at a stile signposted Skyreholme. The path crosses fields above Fir Beck to reach Howarth Farm on Hazler Lane from Appletreewick. Turn right here and into the scattered Norse hamlet of Skyreholme and walk up to the junction where a sign advertises the gardens of Parcevall Hall, seventeenth-century home of the Yorke family and now a popular visitor attraction.

Go towards the hall but leave the road just before you reach the bridge across the Skyreholme Beck by a weir. Take the gate on the left (**3**), where a path leads up into the little wooded gorge of Skyreholme Beck, which widens at the site of the former Skyreholme Dam, which burst in 1899.

As you approach the gloomy, cliff-hemmed entrance of Trollers Gill ahead, you have a choice of routes. The more adventurous will want to risk meeting the barghest and follow the now-dry but rocky gill bed into the heart of Trollers Gill. There are no real difficulties and you soon emerge at Gill Heads, where the path taken by the less-adventurous has contoured left, up and round Middle Hill and past the former Gill Head Mine to meet near the pot-hole of Hell Hole.

On reaching the lane from Skyreholme, turn left (**4**) and then right onto the track known as Kail Lane which leads unerringly down for about 1½ miles (2.5km) across Appletreewick Pastures. Kail Hill soon appears ahead, as the lane becomes enclosed and swings round to the right under Dib Side and Ewe Close Scar.

Dropping down past Hartlington Hall, up on the opposite bank of Barben Beck, Kail Lane reaches the Burnsall–Appletreewick road. You cross straight over (**5**) and drop down to the river again at Woodhouse Farm, to rejoin the Dales Way and turn right back to Burnsall Bridge and the village.

The cliff-hemmed entrance to Trollers Gill

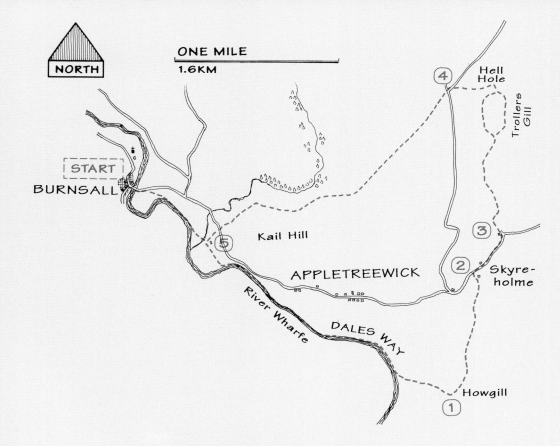

ONE MILE
1.6KM

NORTH

START
BURNSALL

Kail Hill

APPLETREEWICK

River Wharfe

DALES WAY

Hell Hole

Trollers Gill

Skyre-holme

Howgill

④ ③ ② ① ⑤

Map OS Outdoor Leisure Sheet 10, Yorkshire Dales (Southern Area)
Start/Finish Burnsall GR 032611
Length About 8 miles (13km)
Walking time Allow 3–4 hours
Difficulty Easy paths and tracks, with some lane walking and a short discretionary scramble up Trollers Gill

The Route in Brief

Start GR 032611, from village car park in Burnsall. Cross bridge and turn R onto E bank of Wharfe, following Dales Way and sign to Howgill.

1 Follow path S for 2 miles (3.2km) by river, passing Kail Hill and Appletreewick (L) to reach lane at Howgill. Turn L on road then immediately R across stile signed to Skyreholme.

2 Cross fields parallel to Fir Beck and, at Howarth Farm, turn R on lane to Skyreholme.

3 At junction, turn L towards Parcevall Hall then L at gate before bridge, up Skyreholme Beck towards Trollers Gill. Alternative paths take you L above the gill up Middle Hill, or R, up the (dry) bed of the gill.

4 Turn L at Hell Hole to reach lane, and then R onto Kail Lane descending pasture for about 1½ miles (2.5km).

5 Cross road to rejoin the Dales Way at Woodhouse, turning R back to Burnsall.

THE LIMESTONE WONDERS OF WHAFEDALE

Mid-Wharfedale is a limestone lover's paradise. The frowning crag of Kilnsey marks the cut-off point of the Ice Age glacier which created the once lake-filled broad, flat floor of the dale, while the Yorkshire Wildlife Trust's nature reserve of Grass Wood contains an internationally important range of lime-loving wildflowers under its native ash trees. Above this, the crags, scars and pavements of New Close and Conistone contain a wealth of prehistoric settlements and field systems, deserted medieval villages and some oddities like the extraordinary outcrop known as Conistone Pie.

This long day's walk, linking the 'capital of Wharfedale', Grassington, with Kettlewell, 6 miles (10km) up the dale, is mostly easy walking on a grassy terrace which picks its high-level way between the scars with outstanding views across to Kilnsey, returning via the riverside village of Conistone.

From the large car park in Grassington, turn left into the village and left into Chapel Street, which drops down to Town Head. At a sharp turn left in the road, continue straight on through a farmyard on a path signposted to Conistone.

This is the Dales Way, and it ascends steadily (**1**) through the humps and hollows of the sites of two deserted medieval villages to the open field of Lea Green. Continue north above, with Grass Wood below you to the left above Dib Beck and the limestone pavements of Dib Pasture to cross Scot Gate Lane, running up from the village of Conistone below.

There are good views from here of hooded Kilnsey Crag, across the water meadows of the Wharfe with High Ox Pasture rising behind. A few yards beyond the lane, you pass the strange limestone outcrop known as Conistone Pie on the left – and it does look exactly like a crusty pie, the funnel sticking up in the middle to keep the 'pastry' up. There's a grand view from its cairn-topped summit across to Kilnsey and

The great hooded cowl of Kilnsey Crag dominates mid-Wharfedale

Kettlewell, on the banks of the Wharfe, from the bottom of Gate Cote Scar

north to the junction of the Wharfe with Littondale and the Skirfare at Amerdale Dub below Knipe Scar. (Amerdale was the old name for Littondale.)

Passing above Swineber Scar, the path continues on its almost level course to join Highgate Leys Lane on the edge of the conifer plantation of Crookacre Wood. Turn left here (**2**) and drop down to the valley road, turning right towards Kettlewell. At Crookacre Barn, take the stile on the right (**3**) which leads the Dales Way across the fields to Kettlewell.

After exploring this charming Wharfeside village, retrace your steps down the dale, this time with entirely different views, to Scot Gate Lane, where you turn right (**4**) to drop down Wassa Bank past the TV mast on Wassa Hill onto the valley road again, turning left into Conistone.

Passing through the pleasant little village of Conistone ('the king's manor') with its little towerless church of St Mary's looking like it ought to be in the Lake District, you pass the road turning right to Conistone Bridge. But you must continue south until you reach a footpath sign to Grassington, leading off to the left (**5**).

This is followed as it ascends the meadows below the prominent limestone scars and around a buttress on a terrace and down into Dib Beck. Out the other side, the path winds up between the scars back to the large open pasture of Lea Green, above Grass Wood, now on your right. Contouring above the wood, you will soon reach your outward path, which is followed back down into Grassington.

Map OS Outdoor Leisure Sheet 10, Yorkshire Dales (Southern Area)

Start/Finish Grassington GR 002637

Length About 13 miles (21km)

Walking time Allow at least 6 hours

Difficulty Good paths all the way and no major climbs

The Route in Brief

Start GR 002637, from the car park in Grassington, turning L and L again into Chapel Street down to Town Head. Where it turns L, go straight ahead through farm, signposted Conistone.

1 Follow Dales Way (N) above Grass Wood, crossing Lea Green to Dib Beck, crossed by a ladder stile, to cross Scot Gate Lane. Continue N through limestone scars, passing Conistone Pie (L).

2 At Highgate Leys Lane, turn L down to meet road, turning R to Kettlewell.

3 Turn R across stile at Crookacre Barn, across fields into Kettlewell.

4 Retrace steps to Scot Gate Lane, where you turn R and descend to road, turning L into Conistone.

5 Go through village and turn L after junction leading to bridge to follow path signed Grassington, up and above Grass Wood to rejoin outward track at Lea Green.

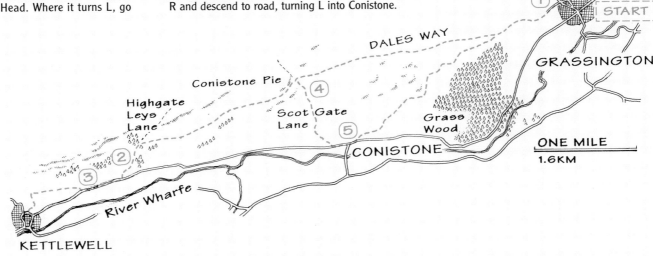

HEBDEN'S LEADEN LEGACY

The lead boom which swept through the Dales during the eighteenth and nineteenth centuries was not confined to Swaledale. Anywhere in the limestone dales where the precious galena (lead ore) could be found became fair game for the prospectors, and Hebden Gill, above the Wharfe on the southern edge of the rich Grassington field, was no exception.

According to Ella Pontefract's *Wharfedale*, Hebden's lead miners had one of the most beautiful journeys home after their hard day's labour in the mines around the head of Hebden Gill.

It is a green, wooded gill, living up to its name which means 'hip valley', and making a lovely setting for Black Scar waterfall in its midst... Willows line the banks of the beck, and early in the winter their branches turn a deep wine colour, and keep this warm tone in the surrounding grey till the buds shoot in the spring.

We follow in the footsteps of Hebden's lead miners in this easy afternoon's stroll from the village, which, like its larger neighbour Grassington, stands away from the river on its western bank.

Walk north from the Town Hill end of the village and take the lane which leads up the left (western) side of Hebden Beck, past High green and Knowles Lathe to reach the hamlet of Hole Bottom after about ¾ of a mile (1.2km). Here, turn right (**1**) over a footbridge across the beck, then follow the miners' track through spoil heaps and ruined buildings upstream.

This track is followed past a small reservoir and Black Scar waterfall to a ford where Bolton Gill joins the beck from the right. Turn right here up the gill (**2**), noting the remains of a winding shaft and the three pillars above a water channel or 'sough' used to drain the mines above.

Now turn right again on a path which leads off across the slopes southwards. This easy,

The bridge across Hebden Beck at Hole Bottom
Left: Dusk over Mossy Moor Reservoir above
Hebden Gill

fairly level path is followed towards the wall of
Mossy Moor Reservoir, which is passed on the
left. The path leads down past a small prehistoric stone circle of eight stones, nearly hidden
in the heather of Mossy Moor to the left.

At Scar Top House, you have a choice of
routes back to Hebden. Either (**3**) turn right
following a complex route which passes Scar
Top House on your left, dropping down
through Care Scar to bear left following a wall
across the fields back to Hebden. Alternatively
(**4**), keep straight on across Edge Top to drop
down to the B6265 at High Dene, turning right
for Hebden.

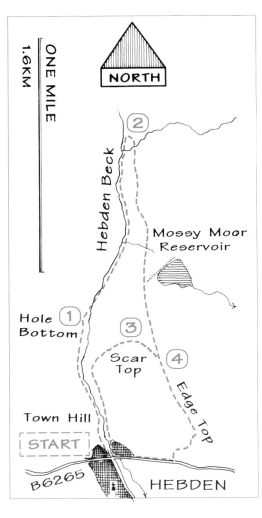

NORTH

ONE MILE
1.6KM

Hebden Beck

Mossy Moor
Reservoir

②

Hole ①
Bottom

③

Scar
Top

④

Edge Top

Town Hill

START

B6265

HEBDEN

FACT FILE

Map OS Outdoor Leisure Sheet 10, Yorkshire
Dales (Southern Area)
Start/Finish Hebden GR 026631
Length ³/₄ mile (1.2km)
Walking time Allow 2 hours
Difficulty An easy afternoon stroll

The Route in Brief

Start GR 026631, from Hebden walk N up Town
Hill, to take lane leading up L (W) side of Hebden
Beck.
1 At Hole Bottom, continue up beck by track over
bridge to Bolton Gill.
2 Turn R then R again on mostly level path past
Mossy Moor Reservoir and across Mossy Ridge to
Scar Top.
3 Turn R at stile, bearing L after passing Scar Top
House and drop down back into Hebden.
(**4** Alternatively, continue S from Scar Top to
Edge Top to drop down to B6265 at High Dene,
turning R back to Hebden.)

THE ASCENT OF BUCKDEN PIKE

The pretty stone village of Buckden owes its existence on the pleasant west-facing slopes of mighty Buckden Pike to the medieval hunting forest of Langstrothdale Chase. There's a clue in the name, which in Old English meant the valley of the bucks, and upper Wharfedale is still known on the map as Langstrothdale. Forest lodges are recorded at Hubberholme, Yockenthwaite, Beckermonds and Oughtershaw. Buckden was set up as a foresters' village after the Domesday Survey, probably by the de Romilles and Cliffords of Skipton Castle, who not only hunted deer but also wild boar and otter in the wild upper parts of the dale.

The ascent of Buckden Pike (2302ft/ 702m) from Buckden is a classic Dales walk, and affords wonderful views down the dale, west to Three Peaks country and down into the hidden reaches of Waldendale to the north-west.

From the large village car park, take the gate which leads directly north into Buckden Rake, contouring gently up through the trees of Rakes Wood. Looking back (south) note the ruler-straight enclosure walls which march in parallel up the fellside, ignoring the stepped profile of the hill.

Leaving Rakes Wood behind, you are now on the Roman road which linked their forts at Ilkley with Bainbridge in Wensleydale. There are fine views here north-west to the head of the dale beyond Hubberholme and into the heart of the old forest of Langstrothdale.

Turn right (**1**) onto an indistinct path which leads steeply up the fellside through a series of gates until the open fell is reached. After the last gate, you head up to the wall coming up from the left, which is followed to the summit. The views from here are among the most extensive in the Dales, to the giants of Pen-y-ghent and Ingleborough across the intervening Birks Fell to the west, to the Nidderdale and Masham Moors to the east, and an intimate glimpse into forgotten Waldendale to the north-west.

Follow the wall south from the summit to the memorial cross to the Polish airmen whose aircraft crashed on the summit in January 1942. Descending now, pass through a gate (**2**) and down onto Walden Road, an old packhorse

Mid-summer in a cottage garden at Starbotton
Left: The memorial cross to Polish airmen near the summit of Buckden Pike

route which linked Wharfedale with the head of Waldendale and into Wensleydale. Alternatively, you can continue south over Tor Mere Top and down into Starbotton via the Starbotton Cam Road.

Walden Road descends the southern spur of Buckden Pike, above the deep ravine of Cam Gill Beck to the left, with fine views ahead down the length of Wharfedale and into Starbotton. Turn left through the village, and then right (**3**) as the last buildings are passed, onto an enclosed track which leads down to a footbridge across the Wharfe.

Turn right over the bridge (**4**), to follow the river upstream on the Dales Way on the west (left) bank for about 2 miles (3.2km) back to Buckden Bridge.

Map OS Outdoor Leisure Sheet 30, Yorkshire Dales (Northern and Central Areas)
Start/Finish Buckden GR 942774
Length 8 miles (13km)
Walking time Allow 5 hours
Difficulty Good moorland paths with gentle ascents/descents

The Route in Brief

Start GR 942774, from large village car park, by gate which leads directly into Buckden Rake.

1 Bear R soon after leaving Rakes Wood, following path for about 2 miles (3.2km), contouring up through fields, following final wall coming up from L to summit.

2 Cross wall and follow it R past Memorial Cross to meet Walden Road coming up from R at gate. Turn R down Walden Road to Starbotton.

3 Turn L through village and on leaving it, take enclosed lane on R which leads down to footbridge over river.

4 Turn R onto Dales Way for 2 miles (3.2km) back to Buckden.

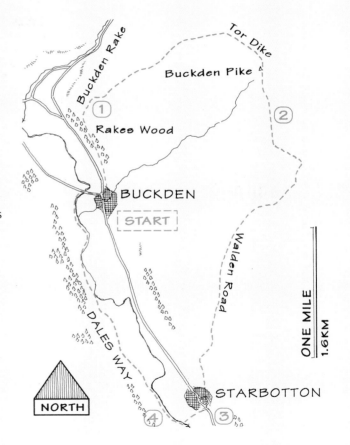

GREAT WHERNSIDE – MONARCH OF WHARFEDALE

G reat Whernside's 2308ft/704m summit is the highest in Wharfedale and also represents a formidable barrier at the head of Nidderdale. It gets its Old English name 'Quernside' from 'the hillside from which millstones were quarried' and the immense square-cut gritstone boulder field which crowns its long, whaleback summit must have been a fruitful source.

Kettlewell, Scandinavian for a stream in a narrow valley, is the starting point for a tough, all-day traverse of Great Whernside's desolate summit, crossing a mysterious Dark Age boundary and returning by an ancient packhorse route.

From the village centre, head west past the church and turn right into a lane which leads alongside the beck which is crossed by a foot-bridge. Turn right on the path up the green

Blackfell Top, the northern summit of Great Whernside, in the distance

Dowber Gill Beck (**1**) on its left bank for about 1½ miles (2.5km), past some pretty waterfalls to Providence Pot. This is a famous pot-hole in the middle of the beck, now covered by an incongruous concrete manhole cover.

Turn right here (**2**) into Dowber Gill Wham, passing the remains of Providence Lead Mine above the beck and to the right. The going gets rougher now as you climb out of the limestone and onto the gritstone moorland. As you get your first view into the head of Nidderdale, with the reservoirs of Angram and Scar House ahead, turn north (**3**) across the moor towards the southern end of Great Whernside, prominent on your left.

Scramble up through the boulders of Long Crag and you are soon at the white trig point which marks the summit of Great Whernside. There is a wild aspect from here, extending to Buckden Pike close by to the north, to the Three Peaks and, best of all, down into upper Nidderdale across the reservoirs of Angram and Scar House.

Continue north along Long Crag to the wall which runs up from Black Dike. Follow this to the left (**4**) to reach the earthworks of Tor Dike, a Dark Age boundary which defended the route into Coverdale. This runs down to the Coverdale road, linking Kettlewell and Leyburn.

If you are feeling fit, you can extend the walk to Tor Mere Top another mile to the west from here, but it can be a rather boggy alternative across some very peaty wastes.

Cross the road at its highest point (**5**) at Little Hunters Sleets, and take the Starbotton Road track due west. At the junction with the green lane of Top Mere Road (**6**), Kettlewell is signposted to the left.

All that is left now is an easy, 2 mile (3.2km) descent across Cam Pasture on a stone-walled track to meet the Coverdale road on a bend just above the village. Turn right to Kettlewell.

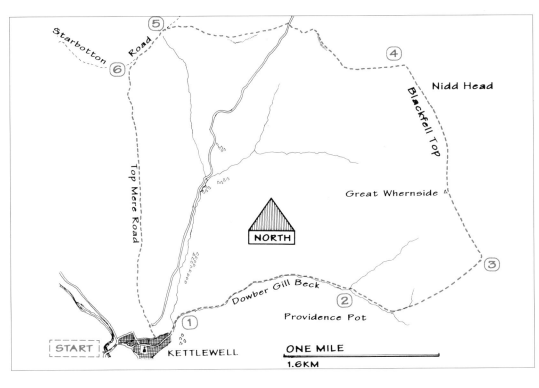

FACT FILE

Map OS Outdoor Leisure Sheet 30, Yorkshire Dales (Northern and Central Areas)
Start/Finish Kettlewell GR 968723
Length About 8 miles (13km)
Walking time About 4–5 hours
Difficulty Rough moorland 'bogtrotting' for the well-equipped, starting on easy paths and ending on a good track

The Route in Brief

Start GR 968723, from the car park in Kettlewell, and head into village. Go past church and turn sharp R onto lane alongside beck which is crossed by a footbridge.

1 Turn R on path up Dowber Gill Beck at a gate.

2 Follow beckside path for 1½ miles (2.5km) to Providence Pot, taking the R branch into Dowber Gill Wham.

3 When the view to Nidderdale opens out veer L (due N), climbing across rough moorland to the boulders and trig point on Great Whernside summit.

4 Head N from summit ridge, then NNW following wall down to Tor Dike and Coverdale road.

5 Cross road and follow Tor Dike to join Starbotton Road and junction with Top Mere Road.

6 Turn L and follow Top Mere Road back down to Kettlewell.

2

NIDDERDALE:
DALE OF LOST OPPORTUNITY

Nidderdale is the Yorkshire Dales in microcosm. In its quiet, unassuming way it has all the attributes which have made the Dales famous: wild, open moorland; dramatic limestone gorges, caves and pot-holes; weirdly sculpted rocks, and ancient, flower-decked stone villages.

Yet when the Yorkshire Dales National Park was designated in 1954, Nidderdale was inexplicably excluded. The reason, according to the bureaucrats, was that the three reservoirs which flood its upper reaches had spoiled the 'natural' environment, and the interests of the water industry prevailed.

More recently, most of Upper Nidderdale was made an Area of Outstanding Natural Beauty (AONB), a second-tier designation in landscape protection terms. But to anyone who has ever visited this special place, the belated AONB designation does not do justice to this beautiful dale. Local resident and landscape historian Dr Richard Muir has rightly described Nidderdale as 'the dale of lost opportunity'.

Without the strict planning protection that only National Park status can give, Nidderdale

The Blacksmith Rock at Brimham Rocks

has started to suffer from the blight of creeping suburbia, with brash and insensitive housing estates springing up in places like Hampsthwaite and Darley. Fortunately, the upper part of the dale beyond its 'capital' of Pateley Bridge has so far largely escaped this fate, and this is where some of the best walking is to be found.

Nidderdale, according to our old friend Alfred Brown, is 'the gentlest of the great dales, a dale made for poets and lovers, with a pastoral beauty which is second to none'. It provides a gentle, sylvan introduction to the greater dales of the Wharfe and Swale, for the first thing which strikes the visitor entering the dale from the south is the abundance of trees. From the mock-Elizabethan estate village of Ripley at the foot of the dale, through the string of one-time industrial hamlets of Smelthouses, Summerbridge and Glasshouses, the Nidd is largely hidden by lush banks of billowing trees.

The Celtic name of the Nidd means brilliant or shining, and the best way to appreciate the accuracy of that ancient description is to follow the Nidderdale Way, which marches the length of the river. I treasure the memory of a family

holiday spent in a caravan on the banks of the river at Summerbridge, where we shared the use of the stepping stones across the sparkling Nidd with a pair of curtseying dippers.

Our site was within walking distance of one of the wonders of Nidderdale, the fantastic pile of Brimham Rocks, perhaps the best example in Britain of the results of wind-erosion under desert conditions. The ridge-top 400 acre (162ha) National Trust estate contains as strange a collection of natural rock formations as you will find anywhere in Britain, all carved from the native 300 million-year-old millstone grit bedrock by wind, frost and rain. So amazing are the shapes of its tors, Brimham Rocks was for long thought to be the work of Druids. In 1786, pioneer archaeologist Major Hayman Rooke suggested they must be the work of 'artists skilled in the power of mathematics'.

The identity of the first residents of Pateley Bridge, the charming little market town which is both the hub and focus of the dale, is given away by its name and that of the neighbouring hamlet of Bewerley. Pateley refers to the 'pate', an old name for the badger, while Bewerley is a name associated with the beaver.

Today's residents are mainly hard-working dalesfolk, still dependent on the fortnightly livestock market, first granted in a charter of the early fourteenth century. The Pateley Bridge Show held in September is one of the finest in all the Dales.

Beyond Pateley Bridge, Nidderdale becomes much more remote and rural, and much more like the larger dales. The first of the string of three reservoirs, Gouthwaite, was constructed between 1893 and 1901 to provide water for Bradford. It is one of the most natural-looking reservoirs in the Dales, an impression which may be partly due to the fact that the dam utilises a moraine which presumably once held back a glacial lake. Gouthwaite is famed for its bird life (a real rarity among reservoirs), which can include flocks of teal, wigeon, tufted duck, curlew and goldeneye.

The neat little stone villages of Ramsgill, Lofthouse and Middlesmoor (whose hill-top churchyard provides one of the finest views down the dale) give access to the upper reaches, where bleak moorlands stud the skyline. Just west of the valley road lies another of Nidderdale's hidden surprises, the dramatic little limestone gorge of the How Stean Beck. Undercut rocks provide narrow passageways for its exciting exploration.

The head of the dale is dominated by the twin reservoirs of Angram and Scar House,

Enclosure walls enmesh the slopes of High Bishopside seen from Bewerley Moor above Pateley Bridge

which were built between 1904 and 1936 by a community of 700 navvies who lived in a shanty town near Scar House, of which there is no trace today. Access to the upper reservoirs is by a private waterworks road which passes the impressive open pot-hole of Goyden Pot.

There is parking by the side of both reservoirs, which nestle under the bleak moorland heights of Great and Little Whernside and Meugher, where the Nidd has its birth.

The ridge of Little Whernside, north of Scar House, runs into the sinisterly named Dead Man's Hill where, in 1728, the headless bodies of three Scottish pedlars were discovered buried in the peat. The story is that they were murdered by the owners of a wayside inn at Woodale, lower down the dale.

Just above the beautifully situated hamlet of Ramsgill, a track leads east via Bouthwaite and Lul Beck towards an extensive area of moorland known as Fountains Earth Moor. The name is a clue to its former ownership, for both Bouthwaite, nearby Covill and Lofthouse were all granges run by the all-powerful Cistercian monks of nearby Fountains Abbey.

Although not strictly in Nidderdale but in the neighbouring valley of the River Skell, Fountains Abbey is without doubt one of the finest monastic ruins in Europe, and was recently made a World Heritage Site. The walk through the parklands of Studley Royal to the majestic remains of Fountains Abbey, whose influence spread so far through the Dales, is therefore included without apology.

THE WORK OF DRUIDS?

The bizarre gritstone pillar known as The Eagle is the highest pinnacle at Brimham Rocks

Early visitors just could not believe that the amazing collection of wind- and ice-sculpted rocks at Brimham in Nidderdale were not the work of Man. In common with unexplained wonders in all parts of Britain, the Druids were the favoured perpetrators and many of the extraordinary formations still bear the names of the mysterious Celtic priesthood, such as the Druid's Cave, the Druid's Writing Desk, the Druid's Coffin, the Pulpit and the Idol.

In fact, the 400 acre (162ha) playground of Brimham Rocks, now carefully managed by the National Trust, is perhaps the finest example of wind and frost erosion in Britain. The millstone grit masterpieces of Brimham were formed as a result of thousands of years of rain, wind and frost working on the vertical and horizontal joints in the sandstone.

Our exploration of this fascinating collection of rocks starts from the hamlet of Low Laithe on the main valley road, the B6165 between Ripley and Pateley Bridge, and takes in the attractive wooded valley of Fell Beck.

Opposite the village pub, follow the bridleway past Wise Ing and Low Wood House, where you pass through a gate on the right (1). This superb green lane was once used by the monks of nearby Fountains Abbey and gives the first view of Brimham Rocks on the skyline to the left. It leads through High Wood and out onto the Summerbridge–Ripon road, where you turn left and follow it for a few yards.

You now enter the National Trust's Brimham Rocks estate, (2) on your left. You will want to spend some time exploring these weird rocks rising from the birch, heather and bilberries – they make a wonderful natural playground for children. The imagination of centuries of tourists have given the formations such fanciful names as the Dancing Bear, the Eagle, the Turtle and the Sphinx. But perhaps the most spectacular outcrop of all is the Druid's Idol, a 203 tonne rock perched precariously on a pedestal only a foot in diameter. It can be found on the northernmost edge of the estate. The National Trust's visitor centre is at Brimham House, the former shooting lodge at the centre of the estate, where refreshments and toilets are provided.

Leave the estate by a footpath which

branches off north beyond the house and drops down to a farm track along the edge of the moor. Turn left here (**3**) through woodland and then right on a field path towards North Pasture Farm. Passing through the farm, follow a track over a beck and out onto the Pateley Bridge–Ripon road (B6265). Taking care on this busy road, turn left and drop down to the tiny hamlet of Fell Beck, where the Half Moon Inn is a convenient hostelry for the thirsty.

Leaving the inn, turn left at the first set of farm buildings (Knoll Top) on the left (**4**) and descend by a wall to a stile which leads down through the trees to Fell Beck.

Follow this charming beck-side path through the trees and past the small lake caused by the damming of the stream by former industry. Then take the footbridge (left) and a path which rises out of the beck around Low Wood Farm (**5**) and then head due south into the woods and down to the beck again, crossing it by another footbridge.

Follow this path downstream to the attractive hamlet of Smelthouses, which takes its name from the fact that from the fourteenth century, lead ore from the Yorke family mines was brought here for smelting. Nothing but the name now remains of this former industry.

Turn left over the Fell Beck bridge (**6**) and then right to reach the valley road again at Knox Manor, turning left to return to Low Laithe and your starting point.

FACT FILE

Map OS Landranger Sheet 99, Northallerton and Ripon
Start/Finish Low Laithe, GR 193636
Length 6 miles (10km)
Walking time Allow 3½ hours
Difficulty On good paths for most of the way

The Route in Brief

Start GR 193636. Follow footpath opposite pub past Wise Ing and Low Wood House.
1 Turn R through gate onto green lane which leads through High Wood, and onto Summerbridge–Ripon Road.
2 Turn L into National Trust Brimham Rocks estate.
3 Leave by footpath N of Brimham House, turning L on farm track through woodland then R towards North Pasture Farm. Turn L on B6265 to Fell Beck.
4 Turn L at Knoll Top Farm to descend to Fell Beck.
5 Over footbridge (L) go round Low Wood Farm and then S to Smelthouses.
6 Turn L over bridge and then R to Knox Manor, turning L to return to Low Laithe.

ONE MILE
1.6KM

AROUND THE UPPER NIDD

Nidderdale was apparently excluded from the Yorkshire Dales National Park in 1954 because of the 'unnatural' string of three reservoirs which have flooded its upper valley. This classic moorland circuit of the Upper Nidd, from which all three reservoirs – the Angram, Scar House and Gouthwaite – can be seen, will surely confirm the planners' mistake. Nidderdale is a gem among the dales and although it recently had AONB status conferred upon it, surely deserves the highest possible protection.

This walk from Middlesmoor, the highest village in the dale with a famous view down the dale from its hill-top churchyard, could easily be combined with an outing to another of Nidderdale's scenic highlights, the weird and wonderful limestone How Stean Gorge (entrance charge), which is just across the meadows to the south of our starting point.

From the car park at the upper end of Middlesmoor village, turn right along a lane (**1**) which rapidly turns into the walled, unmade track known as In Moor Lane. This name refers to the fact that it crosses the wastes of In Moor, with its numerous grouse butts, and up past the trig point of Rain Stang (1486ft/453m), which we pass to the west.

It is a gradual climb, with increasingly fine views back down the dale towards Gouthwaite Reservoir, with the bulk of Fountains Earth Moor and Sypeland Crags to the left.

Past Rain Stang, the track descends steeply to the waterworks road round the south shore of Scar House Reservoir, with magnificent views across the valley to Dead Man's Hill and the disused gritstone quarries of Carle Fell, where the stone for the reservoir was obtained. The sinister name of Dead Man's Hill is said to commemorate the finding of the headless bodies of three Scottish tinkers in the peat in 1728.

Turn right (**2**) to cross the Scar House dam wall, the last of the Nidderdale reservoirs to be completed in 1936, and then turn right (**3**) onto the Nidderdale Way which joins the Carle Fell Road which served the quarries above.

This good path contours easily along Carle Fell Side before dropping down into the craggy depths of Woo Gill, which is crossed like Twizling Gill by a ford (**4**). Now head north on a path which winds up Woogill Moor.

Cross Twizling Gill again and climb up on a spoil heap which leads to a prominent old mine shaft joining a good, almost level track.

From the gaping, dripping mouth of the old mine shaft, the rare sight of all three of Nidderdale's reservoirs can be seen – Angram and Scar House nestling below the gullied bulk of Great Whernside and Meugher across Stean Moor, while Gouthwaite occupies a more sylvan setting further down the dale.

This track keeps its line for about 3 miles (5km), offering a grand promenade around the upper reaches of the valley, with magnificent views opening up at every step. As it approaches Dale Edge, an old quarry is passed on the left.

Keeping to the edge of the moor, this splendid track gradually drops down towards the old shooting lodge at Thrope Edge (**5**). This strange building with its separate tower bears a striking resemblance to a church, especially when viewed from the valley road beneath.

Just before reaching the lodge, turn right on a path which zigzags steeply down to Thrope Farm, beyond which you cross the Nidd to join the waterworks road which threads through the valley. You have just crossed Nidderdale's limestone belt and just upstream from here are two of the dale's most famous pot-holes – Goyden Pot and Manchester Hole.

Follow the road to the left as far as a signposted stile on the right (**6**), which leads across the fields and through the narrow woodland of Intake Gill to re-enter Middlesmoor by the hill-top church of St Chad's, completely but tastefully re-built on what appears to be an ancient site in 1866.

Home-spun philosophy on a gravestone in Middlesmoor churchyard
Opposite: Above the Scar House dam, Nidderdale

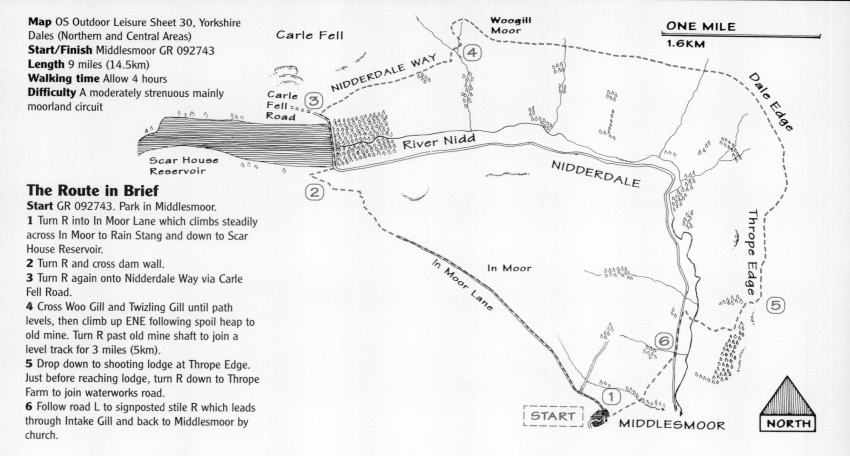

Map OS Outdoor Leisure Sheet 30, Yorkshire Dales (Northern and Central Areas)
Start/Finish Middlesmoor GR 092743
Length 9 miles (14.5km)
Walking time Allow 4 hours
Difficulty A moderately strenuous mainly moorland circuit

The Route in Brief

Start GR 092743. Park in Middlesmoor.
1 Turn R into In Moor Lane which climbs steadily across In Moor to Rain Stang and down to Scar House Reservoir.
2 Turn R and cross dam wall.
3 Turn R again onto Nidderdale Way via Carle Fell Road.
4 Cross Woo Gill and Twizling Gill until path levels, then climb up ENE following spoil heap to old mine. Turn R past old mine shaft to join a level track for 3 miles (5km).
5 Drop down to shooting lodge at Thrope Edge. Just before reaching lodge, turn R down to Thrope Farm to join waterworks road.
6 Follow road L to signposted stile R which leads through Intake Gill and back to Middlesmoor by church.

FOUNTAINS ABBEY AND STUDLEY ROYAL

Although not strictly in Nidderdale, few visitors to the dale will want to miss what is the finest monastic ruin in Britain, arguably in Europe, and a superb, romantic walk. Fountains Abbey and its enclosing parkland of Studley Royal is a World Heritage Site and one of the most visited sites in the care of its owners, the National Trust.

The intense pressure of traffic on the narrow valley road from Ripon and Pateley Bridge has unfortunately robbed modern visitors of the dramatic introduction to the abbey which formerly was enjoyed on the valley approach past Fountains Hall. Instead, visitors have to start from the ugly, barn-like (but needless-to-say, award-winning) new Visitors Centre, on the high ground north of the abbey. All the usual accoutrements are there, a restaurant, shop, audio-visual show and exhibition, but the first sight of the abbey tower – a sadly truncated view of its topmost portion – just cannot compare with the former introduction.

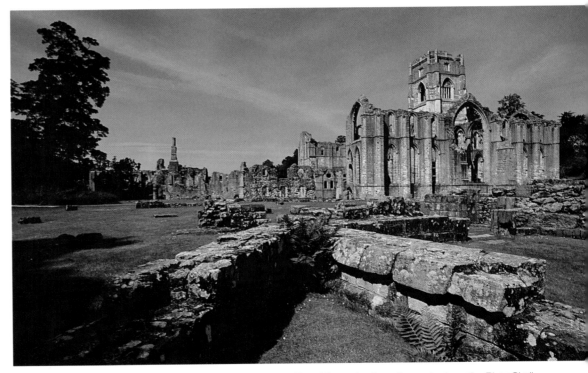

The abbey ruins from the east, along the River Skell

Descend the engineered path known as the Clifftop Walk, with its aerial viewpoints, to the abbey itself, which is somehow diminished by this approach. You need to spend some time just wandering around the magnificent cloisters, soaring arches and time-worn steps of this wonderful building, a monument to the single-minded dedication and piety of the powerful Cistercian monks, who built it on the wealth won from their extensive estates throughout the Dales nearly nine centuries ago.

Walk along the broad path which runs east (**1**) following the River Skell and past the small overgrown quarries from which much of the stone for the abbey was won. Eventually, this easy path turns up through the ornamental trees and shrubs at Tent Hill and ascends up to the romantic pile of the Banqueting House, standing proudly on its manicured lawn.

From here, the path turns right and returns to the broad track by the Canal, with fine views through the yews of the Water Gardens below. Walk up to the Canal Gates entrance and car park. Turn left (**2**) and walk through the deer park of Studley Royal to the ornate little church of St Mary's. Built in high Victorian Gothic style by William Burges between 1871–78 for the 1st Marquess of Ripon, it has a strikingly colourful and decorated interior, well worth an inspection.

Retrace your steps back to the Canal Gates entrance and cross the bridge over the Cascade, bearing right up the steep path,

The Octagon Tower from the gardens of Studley Royal
Left: The soaring tracery of Fountains Abbey

40

which plunges into the Serpentine Tunnel to emerge just below the pinnacled Octagon Tower. Walk on through the trees (**3**) past the Temple of Fame (whose white 'stone' columns are actually made of wood) and up to the Surprise View and Anne Boleyn's Seat – and a fine view of the valley of the Skell, with the abbey nestling elegantly in the valley below, best seen in the winter when the leaves are off the trees.

After admiring the view, descend through the trees back to the Half Moon Pond, created like the rest of the gardens by William Aislabie during the eighteenth century. Turn left (**4**) on reaching the main path, and return to the abbey along the southern bank of the Skell.

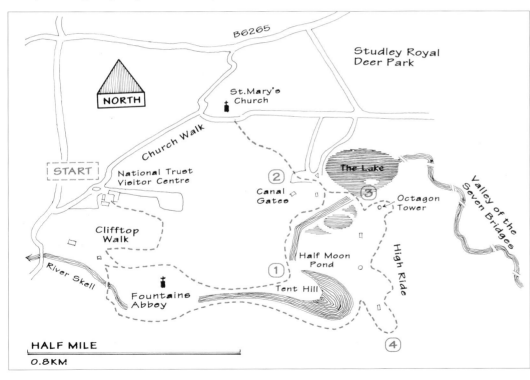

FACT FILE

Map OS Pathfinder 653, Fountains Abbey and Boroughbridge
Start/Finish National Trust Visitor Centre, GR 273686
Length About 2¹/₂ miles (4km)
Walking time Allow at least 3 hours
Difficulty Easy lowland walking on good paths

The Route in Brief

Start GR 273686, at the new National Trust Visitor Centre, N of the Abbey ruins. Follow engineered path down to Abbey in valley of the River Skell.
1 Follow path E through meadows to Tent Hill, then up through trees past the Canal to the Banqueting House.
2 From the Canal Gates entrance car park, turn sharp L to walk through the deer park of Studley Royal to St Mary's Church.
3 Return to car park and cross the Canal where it exits The Lake and ascend through trees to the Octagon Tower, Temple of Fame and Surprise View.
4 Descend to Half Moon Pond, and follow broad path on S bank of the Skell back to the Abbey and Visitor Centre.

3

MALHAMDALE:
SCAR, TARN AND GORGE

Little do they know it, but the thousands of visitors who cram into Malham every summer weekend are merely following in the footsteps of the first settlers of this lovely limestone dale.

Seven thousand years ago, after the last of the Ice Age glaciers had finally retreated, the first Mesolithic hunter-gatherers ventured across the land bridge which still existed between Britain and the Continent in search of food.

We know that they reached Malham because hundreds of their tiny flint implements, known as microliths, have been found scattered around the shores of Malham Tarn and several other now-drained tarns, or picked up from molehills in the area.

But these Middle Stone Age people would only have ventured this far north in a good summer season, when the sun glinted brightly off the white walls of Malham's limestone scars and crags, and their prey emerged from the wildwood. In that way, as the great Dales historian, Dr Arthur Raistrick, has pointed out, they are exactly like today's caravanners and

campers, and could accurately be described as the dale's first summer visitors.

There can be little doubt that those Mesolithic hunters would have held Malhamdale's magnificent landscape features, such as Malham Cove and Gordale Scar, in much the same measure of awe and wonder as the sensitive modern visitor does.

'To them,' wrote Dr Raistrick in his masterful 1947 survey of *Malham and Malham Moor*, 'each piece of wild scenery would be peopled by spirits, some friendly, some to be feared and propitiated. Each stream and waterfall, rocky crag and sheltered woody hollow would have its native spirit and its accumulated tradition.'

And he added with the perception of a true poet 'What a vast procession of friendly ghosts must haunt the village on quiet nights if we allow our imagination to work in such terms. Tall, fair men of the Bronze Age; smaller, darker men of the Celtic Brigantes, the sturdy "hill-men", independent, defying the Romans; Angles, Danes, Norsemen; farmers, shepherds, monks and miners. All have lived and worked here and left their traces on the ground.'

It is impossible to walk over the bright, emerald pastures of Malham or to clatter across the clints and grikes of its fretted limestone pavements without recalling that continuing sense of history. Indeed, the high, relatively dry limestone fells north of the Mid-Craven fault which created Malham's scenic wonders were much more heavily populated during prehistoric times than they are today, as a glance at the map will show. The Gothic lettering indicating 'settlements', 'field systems' and 'hut circles' shows that a vigorous agriculture was being practiced here during the Bronze and Iron Ages. This was continued by the monks of Fountains and Bolton Abbeys, who ran most of Malham Moor as a vast, empty sheep ranch from their granges at Kilnsey and Malham during the Middle Ages.

But it is the natural wonders which attract most of today's visitors to Malham, as they have ever since the earliest tourists like William Wordsworth first described and popularised Malham's Cove and Tarn, and Gordale Scar. Wordsworth's description of the Cove 'Tier under tier, this semicirque profound' has hardly been bettered since, although no one will

ever know for sure whether, as is claimed, the sooty lichen stains were the inspiration for Charles Kingsley's falling chimney-sweep in *The Water Babies*. Today's Cove cliff-hangers are the rock athletes whose exploits defy gravity and, some would say, commonsense.

The dry valley beyond the Cove, known as Watlowes, winds for a dramatic half mile between scars and clints towards the enigmatic expanse of Malham Tarn, a natural lake in the heart of leaky limestone country. The reason for this oddity is that it lies on a bed of impervious Silurian slate brought to the surface by the North Craven Fault. The water is impounded by a glacial moraine and is famous for the richness of its wildlife, which has been investigated for many years by students at the Field Study Centre at Tarn House.

It is only on very rare occasions today that visitors are treated to the impressive sight of water from the Tarn spilling over the 300ft (90m) high lip of the Cove, as it did in prehistoric times. According to Mr Hurtley, the old but rather ungrammatical Malham schoolmaster in the late eighteenth century, it made 'a more grand and magnificent Cascade than imagination can form an idea of'.

Although many guidebooks still perpetuate the myth, the crystal stream which bubbles from beneath the impending wall of Malham Cove is

not the infant River Aire, nether does it come, as it logically should, from Malham Tarn above. The Aire and the tarn's waters actually dive under the Cove to rise at Aire head Springs, half a mile south of Malham village.

Two impressive waterfalls still exist in the upper reaches of neighbouring Gordale Scar, which was formed similarly to the Cove along the line of Mid-Craven Fault. But Gordale's upper waterfall only burst through the rockface in the 1730s, before which, like Malham's Niagara, it gushed over the lip of the escarpment above. The 'dreadful canopy' of Gordale so impressed the poet Thomas Gray on his visit in 1769 that he could only stay, 'not without shuddering', for a quarter of an hour, and 'thought my trouble richly paid, for the impression will last for life'. Wordsworth famously described it: 'Gordale chasm, terrific as the lair where the young lions crouch'.

Again, there is good exploration to be done in the mile-long dry valley beyond Gordale Scar. According to Dr Raistrick, 'No finer view of a limestone gorge can be obtained than this'.

One other waterfall deserves a mention in this brief description of Malhamdale's highlights. Janet's Foss, between Malham village and Gordale, recalls the ghosts of both the history and mythology of Malham. Janet was queen of the local fairies, who was said to live in a cave behind the wall of tufa over which the lace-like waterfall in Gordale Beck tumbles. And foss, of course, is the Old Norse word for waterfall.

An evening view south over Gordale from New Close Knotts. Note the strip lynchets on Cawden in the middle distance

A MALHAM MEANDER

The area north of Malham village in Upper Airedale is famous for its spectacular limestone landscapes, which represent some of the finest glacio-karst (limestone affected by glaciation) scenery in Britain. The awesome amphitheatre of Malham Cove, topped by its jigsaw-like acres of limestone pavements and the oddity of Malham Tarn, an improbable lake in porous limestone country, makes this a favourite destination for school geology trips. But all these natural attractions mean that Malham is a place to be avoided in high summer when the school parties and trippers take over. Save your visit until autumn or winter and you will have a different Malham, elemental and magnificent, virtually to yourself. This easy 5 miles (8km) walk is a gentle introduction to the wonders of Malham.

Start from the main village car park near the Dales National Park Visitor Centre, turning into the village and keeping left at the junction of the bridge which crosses the Malham Beck. Climbing up the lane through Town Head, you turn right through a gate (1) near the top of the lane signed Malham Cove which is now visible ahead.

Follow this engineered path through the valley below the Cove, and take the left-hand alternative near its foot (2) which leads to a man-made staircase up the left-hand side of the sweeping 300ft (90m) limestone cliff of the Cove. Sometimes you can spy climbers clinging to the face like flies to a wall.

At the top, turn right across the extensive area of limestone pavement which crowns the cove. The view down Malhamdale and Airedale from here is magnificent, and you can pick out the 'staircases' of the early cultivation terraces known as strip lynchets on Shorkley Hill down the valley to the left. Malham Cove lies on the line of the Middle Craven Fault, a major fracture in the Great Scar limestone which runs east to west across the Dales. Glacial action and the scouring effects of meltwater polished these imposing rocks into today's impressive landforms.

Cross the top of the Cove with care because it is easy to break or twist an ankle on the clints and grikes, and follow the wall which leads directly away from the Cove (3), across an intervening wall by a stile.

This leads into the dry valley known as Watlowes, along which, shortly after the end of the Ice Age, a mighty river flowed to pour over the lip of Malham Cove in a waterfall higher than Niagara. The crags and scars of Watlowes

The dizzy view from the eastern buttress of Malham Cove

45

Map Outdoor Leisure Sheet 10 Yorkshire Dales (Southern Area)
Start/Finish Malham Car Park, GR 900627
Length 5 miles (8km)
Walking time Allow 3 hours
Difficulty Easy walking in general, but rocky paths in Watlowes

The Route in Brief

Start GR 900627. From the large car park walk through the village, keeping L at the junction by the bridge to Town Head.
1 Near the top of the lane, turn R through a gate signposted Malham Cove.
2 Approaching the Cove, turn L up the man-made staircase to the top and walk towards the centre of the limestone pavements.
3 Follow the wall leading N away from the Cove and into the dry valley of Watlowes.
4 Turn R over a stile under Dean Moor Hill to Water Sinks.
5 At road turn R and then L on the Pennine Way to view Malham Tarn. Retrace steps to the road and turn L.
6 Turn R following Pennine Way signs across Prior Rakes and along Trougate, turning R to return to the top of the Cove.
7 Retrace route back to Malham village.

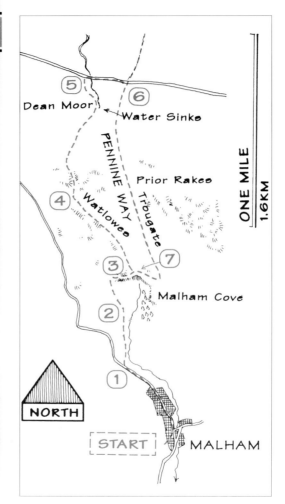

tower above you like a miniature Arizona. At the head of the valley, turn sharp right over a stile (**4**) below Dean Moor Hill.

You now leave the limestone outcrops behind and follow a wall towards Water Sinks. It would be logical to assume that the stream which disappears here is the one which emerges at the foot of Malham Cove, but nothing is quite what it seems in limestone country. The water diving beneath the surface here in fact emerges as the River Aire at Aire Head, half a mile south of Malham village.

When you reach the Settle–Malham road, turn right then left along the Pennine Way (**5**). Soon you will see Malham Tarn, a geological freak explained by the fact that it rests on a bed of impervious slates. On the far side, sheltering in a belt of trees beneath Highfields Scar, is Tarn House, a famous Field Study Centre.

Retrace your route back to the road at Water Sinks Gate, turning left then right (**6**) on the Pennine Way south-bound across the green pastures of Prior Rakes, passing over three walls. The path enters the trough of Trougate, which threads its way between low outcrops of limestone back to the eastern end of Malham Cove by a path leading down to the right.

We now head back towards Malham (**7**) across the top of the Cove down the steps, with another chance to admire the sweeping walls of the Cove from its base. Follow the path by the side of Malham Beck which leads back to the road just above the village. Turn left here to go back through the village to the car park.

PIKEDAW AND NAPPA CROSS

Although overshadowed by the higher hills of Kirkby Fell, Rye Loaf Hill and Grizedales, Pikedaw Hill (1520ft/463m) is nevertheless one of the finest viewpoints in Malhamdale. From the ancient cairn on its rocky summit, you look down across the line of the Mid-Craven Fault towards Malham Cove and Gordale Scar to the east, where the lynchets and settlements of the first farmers in the dale can easily be seen. Medieval Nappa Cross, at the summit of this walk, was originally erected by monks to guide travellers across the moors long before the enclosure commissioners built their network of walls.

The area between Pikedaw and Grizedales was also once a hive of industry. During the 1790s, calamine, a zinc ore used to produce brass but best-known today for its use in a soothing lotion, was discovered here and produced in large quantities. The faint remains of shafts, pits and tips among the scars and pavements on Pikedaw and along the green track down to Langscar Gate can still be seen.

The view north-east from Nappa Cross towards Malham Tarn

Our walk starts from the large car park in Malham, where you turn right up the enclosed track and then immediately left on another which leads into Long Lane.

At Burns Barn (**1**), take the left fork leading directly towards Pikedaw Hill, straight ahead, with Kirkby Fell behind. After the fourth barn on the left, go over the stile on the right (**2**), which climbs above Sell Gill between Pikedaw and Kirkby Fell towards the scar of Hoober Edge, below Pikedaw's summit.

Passing below the edge, turn right for the short scramble to the top of Pikedaw, and the superb view described above. Continue ascending to the north-west, passing a cave as you approach an area of fretted limestone pavement. The path meets the line of Stockdale Lane here, an ancient monastic route between Settle and Malham. Turn left (**3**) through a gate and follow the far side of the wall (right) to climb up to the restored Nappa Cross, the 1675ft (510m) summit of the walk and a fine viewpoint across Malham Moor towards the distant Malham Tarn, nestling below Great Close Hill.

Map OS Outdoor Leisure Sheet 10, Yorkshire Dales (Southern Area)
Start/Finish Malham GR 900627
Length 6 miles (10km)
Walking time Allow 3½ hours
Difficulty Easy limestone pastures and field paths

The Route in Brief

Start GR 900627, from the main car park in Malham village. Turn up the enclosed track on the R, then L into Long Lane.

1 At Burns Barn take the L branch leading towards Pikedaw Hill ahead.

2 After the fourth barn, take the stile which leads R across the Butterlands Barn and head for the scar of Hoober Edge below Pikedaw Hill, which can be ascended from here.

3 From Pikedaw, head N on path which climbs up past a cave (R) to reach Stockdale Lane by a gate near an area of limestone pavement.

4 Turn L through gate and follow wall to Nappa Cross. Follow this track down the fell to meet lane at Langscar Gate.

5 Cross straight over and turn sharp R to follow path downhill, parallel with lane. Rejoin lane, turning R uphill for a short distance, then L onto Long Lane to retrace route back to car park.

Our route follows this old bridleway (**4**) through the area of scars and pavements which produced that precious calamine two centuries ago, to descend to Langscar Gate, on the lane which goes up from Malham to the Cove.

On reaching the lane, pass straight over and join the path (**5**) which leads down parallel to it through the fields with the Cove appearing to the left, rejoining the lane as Malham appears below. Go uphill (right) for a few yards to a sharp bend, where you turn left to rejoin Long Lane and your outward route.

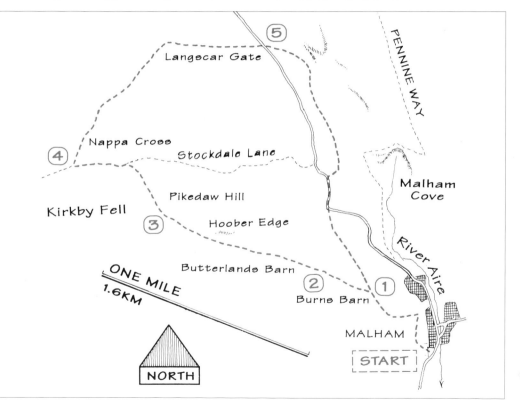

GOTHIC GORDALE AND MONASTIC MASTILES

Thomas Gray graphically described the 'horrors' of Gordale Scar, and the 'dreadful canopy' of its impending walls on his visit in 1769. Ten years later, Adam Walker described the scar as being like a 'promiscuous ruin' (whatever that means!) and equal to anything he had seen in the Alps or Scotland. James Ward's 1812 oil painting of Gordale Scar, now in the Tate Gallery, fashionably emphasises the Gothic horror of Gordale, exaggerating its cliffs and dwarfing a massive White Park bull in the foreground.

Beyond the Georgian hyperbole, Gordale Scar remains a mightily impressive place, its 300ft (90m) cliffs seemingly split asunder by the tiny Gordale Beck, but actually created when it was fed by the powerful meltwaters of a retreating Ice Age glacier.

Above the scar, limestone pastures, crackedand splintered by the ages, are crossed by an ancient green lane, Mastiles Lane, once used by the white-robed monks of Fountains Abbey to link their granges at Kilnsey and Malham. It is a humbling experience to march along back into history, with only the call of the curlew for company.

From Malham car park, walk towards the village but at the bridge over the beck, double back to follow it downstream for a few yards, turning left (**1**) at the stile at Mire Barns to follow Gordale Beck past New Laithe into Wedber Wood. Janet's Foss is a pretty little waterfall embowered in the trees, and the legendary home of Janet, queen of the local fairies, said to live in a cave behind the falling foss.

Turn left out of the trees past the waterfall and up to the lane to Gordale. Turn right, then left over Gordale Bridge through a gate (**2**) which leads to a well-beaten path through meadows towards the impending cliffs of Gordale Scar.

The path passes under the yew-encrusted scars of New Close Knotts and then bends dramatically to the right into the very jaws of Gordale Scar. There are two separate waterfalls in the scar and our route goes up the left-hand side of the lower one (water permitting) by a series of well-worn hand and footholds.

Once past this *mauvais pas*, the path keeps to the left of the chasm, passing the upper falls spouting impressively from an eyehole in the living rock above. Before 1730 apparently, the water fell over a now-defunct waterfall to the left.

Inside the awesome cleft of Gordale Scar

49

A series of steps and paths lead up to the left (3) over the scars and pavements of New Close to emerge at the lane to Malham Tarn beneath the tumulus-crowned eminence of Seaty Hill. Keep right here up to Street Gate, a meeting place of many moorland tracks. Now turn right (4) onto perhaps the most famous of the monastic highways – Mastiles Lane – which crosses Gordale Beck and through the indistinct remains of a Roman camp on a 2 mile (3.2km) trek across the area known as Mastiles.

About half a mile beyond the point where Mastiles Lane becomes enclosed by walls, turn right at a gate (5) which leads off down to the isolated farmstead of Lee Gate, which you pass to the left to enter metalled Smearbottom Lane. Follow this lane for about half a mile, taking the second walled track on the left to climb up to Weets Top, at 1357ft (414m) one of the finest viewpoints in the locality, with an especially fine aerial view of Gordale Scar to the west.

From Weets Top, with its stumpy Cross marking several parish boundaries, take the path (6) leading south down across The Weets and Hanlith Moor into Windy Pike Lane towards Hanlith. At the second sharp left-hand turn in the lane (7) leading down to Hanlith, turn right onto the signposted Pennine Way. This leads round Windy Pike and down to a riverside path back to your outward path and back into Malham.

The ancient trackway of Mastiles Lane, leading west near Bordley

FACT FILE

Map OS Outdoor Leisure Sheet 10, Yorkshire Dales (Southern Area)
Start/Finish Malham GR 900627
Length 10 miles (16km)
Walking time Allow 5–6 hours
Difficulty The ascent of Gordale Scar requires a short but easy rock scramble, which may be slippery after heavy rain. Otherwise, easy tracks, lanes and paths

The Route in Brief

Start GR 900627, from the car park, heading towards village, but after crossing beck, double back S to follow it downstream to a stile.
1 Turn L and follow Gordale Beck upstream to Janet's Foss.
2 From the waterfall, turn L to join Gordale Lane, turning R then L through a gate towards Gordale Scar.
3 Climb the lower waterfall on the L, and keep to the L of gorge to emerge through scars at the lane to Malham Tarn.
4 Follow this to the R to Street Gate and junction with Mastiles Lane. Turn R and follow for about 2 miles (3.2km) to just beyond where walls enclose it on both sides.
5 Turn R here to descend to Lee Gate Farm, joining metalled Smearbottom Lane, taking second track on L to climb up to Weets Top.
6 Descend Hanlith Moor into Windy Pike Lane towards Hanlith.
7 At sharp L bend follow Pennine Way (R) back to Malham.

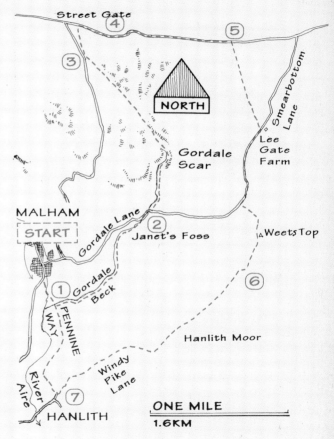

ONE MILE
1.6KM

AIRTON AND KIRKBY MALHAM

Airton is a pretty village of many seventeenth-century cottages clustering around its triangular village green. Prominent in this nonconformist stronghold is the Friends Meeting House of 1700 and the so-called 'squatters' house' on the green. The imposing mill on the River Aire originally spun linen, then cotton, and is now tastefully converted to flats.

This easy four-miler (6.5km) links Airton with its Malhamdale neighbour of Kirkby Malham. The name of this village gives a clue to the fact that its fifteenth-century church of St Michaels is one of the most interesting and attractive in the Dales. There is an ancient preaching cross in its churchyard.

From the village green at Airton, cross the main road and into Hellifield Lane. As you leave the buildings behind, take a gate on the right which leads to Low Croft Barn on Scosthrop Lane. Scosthrop is the scattered settlement to the right, the name literally meaning the village of the Scots.

Turn left (**1**) and follow this lane for about a mile (1.6km), passing an ancient boundary stone on your right. Take the first stile on your right, and cross over the fields between a plantation on the left and Warber Hill on the right (**2**).

Follow the wall (**3**) heading north from Warber Hill which descends to a stile, with good views ahead towards the grey limestone hills of Malham and Gordale. Bear right across the fields at the end of the wall, towards the trees of Kirkby Beck, where you cross a footbridge to enter the village.

Turn right over the crossroads in the village

Deepdale Barns, between Airton and Kirkby Malham
Left: Approaching Kirkby Malham along Green Gate
Lane

(**4**) and down the lane called Green Gate towards Hanlith Bridge over the River Aire. Cross it and turn immediately right by a stile (**5**) onto the Pennine Way (south-bound), which is followed for just over a mile (1.6km) on its riverside path all the way back to Airton.

As you approach Airton, you cross a footbridge over the river and then the mill leat. The path now runs between the mill leat and the river until the former cotton mill is reached and passed to the right.

FACT FILE

Map OS Outdoor Leisure Sheet 10, Yorkshire Dales (Southern Area)
Start/Finish Airton GR 903592
Length Just over 4 miles (6.5km)
Walking time Allow 2½ hours
Difficulty An easy evening stroll with no difficulties

The Route in Brief

Start GR 903592, from Airton's village green over the main road, taking the lane to Hellifield. Leaving the buildings, take the gate on R, which leads to Low Croft Barn on Scosthrop Lane.
1 Turn L and follow lane for about 1 mile (1.6km).
2 Take first stile on your R which leads between a small plantation on L and Warber Hill (R).
3 Follow wall dropping down to a stile, then take path across field to plantation and bear R to Kirkby Beck and across a footbridge into Kirkby Malham.
4 Turn R over the crossroads and into Green Gate leading to Hanlith Bridge.
5 Turn R over bridge and onto the Pennine Way which leads directly S by river and mill leat back to Airton.

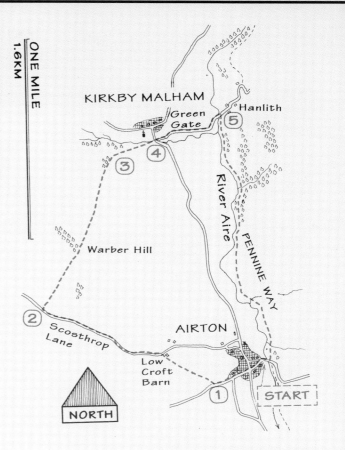

RIBBLESDALE: THREE PEAKS COUNTRY

Ingleborough, Whernside and Penyghent
Are the highest hills twixt Tweed and Trent.
OLD YORKSHIRE RHYME

Wild Ribblesdale – once proposed as a separate 'wilderness zone' at the heart of the Yorkshire Dales National Park – will always be known to walkers as 'Three Peaks Country'. Dominated by the eponymous peaks of Whernside, Pen-y-ghent and Ingleborough, Ribblehead is a wild moorland waste of peat-bog and small limestone outcrops, where the only apparent sign of civilisation is the sweeping, twenty-four-arch Batty Moss viaduct on the monumental Settle–Carlisle line. When seen from the 2414ft (736m) summit of Whernside, far from taming the wildness of its setting, the lace-like viaduct somehow only manages to emphasise the fragility and impermanence of Man's presence in this bleak and inhospitable country.

The trio of Yorkshire's most prized summits have always exerted a powerful influence on walkers and on those who prefer to admire

Winter on drumlins at Beecroft,
near Horton-in Ribblesdale

them from the dales. In 1810, geographer John Bigland claimed unequivocally in his work *A Geographical and Historical View of the World*, that 'The mountains of Craven in Yorkshire, especially Whamside, Pennygant and Ingleborough are the highest in England'. He gave their heights as Whernside 4,050ft; Ingleborough, 3,987ft; and Pen-y-ghent, 3,930ft. But he also quoted a Mr Ewart, a Lancaster mathematician, who had calculated the height of Ingleborough at 2,375ft, which wasn't too far out from its actual 2373ft (723m). Pen-y-ghent, which presents such a noble profile when seen from Horton-in-Ribblesdale, is actually 2273ft (694m).

The classic 26-mile (42km) Three Peaks Walk, which links the three summits in a long day, is an irresistible challenge to many hill-walkers. But it has caused horrendous problems of erosion to the hard-pressed Yorkshire Dales National Park authority, which has spent well over £1 million on path restoration on the route over recent years. For that reason, and the fact that there is plenty of other good walking in Ribblesdale, it will not be featured in this book.

The Three Peaks show to perfection the famous Yoredale Series of Carboniferous rocks which form the basis of Dales geology. Resting on the oldest beds of limestone, the regular succession of shale and gritstone gives the Three Peaks their distinctive, stepped appearance, usually topped by a weather-resistant summit of grit, acting just like the traditional tweed flat cap so loved by the Dales farmer. The limestone bedrock is seen to best effect in the scars, crags and pavements of Attermire, Moughton, Twistleton, in the dramatic little dry valley of Trow Gill; or at Norber, near Austwick, where massive, dark boulders of Silurian slate have been transported by Ice Age glaciers to rest incongruously on the limestone plateau.

The limestone also gives birth to Ribblesdale's famous pot-hole country, where some of the best-known sporting caves in the country are to be found. These range from the open maws of Gaping Gill and Hull and Hunt Pots which yawn enticingly on Ingleborough's and Pen-y-ghent's flanks, to the shallower Victoria and Jubilee Caves, on Attermire Scar near Settle, where evidence has been found of Stone Age occupation. The show caves of White Scar and Ingleborough Cave in Clapdale are much safer

and are justly popular with tourists.

Ingleborough is probably the best-known and most-climbed mountain in all the Broad Acres of Yorkshire. Here on the broad, flat summit of millstone grit is the site of a 15 acre (6ha) hill-fort which may have been the settlement known to the Romans as Rigodunum, where the Brigantian leader Venutious held out with typical Yorkshire grit against the invaders from the Mediterranean. The view from the summit is one of the Dales' finest and extends as far as the Lakeland hills and Morecambe Bay.

Other 'steps' of resistant slate are the cause of the fine series of waterfalls in the beds of the rivers Doe and Twiss at Ingleton, where a charming short walk ends in the highlight of Thornton Force, one of the finest settings for a waterfall in the Dales. Dr Arthur Raistrick defied anyone to place a hand between the limestone of the upper part of the falls and the upturned edge of Cambrian slates on which they rest, and not feel the 'terrifying' unimaginable geological time gap of about 300 million years between the two types of rock.

Whernside is the highest of the Three Peaks, and the second-highest mountain in Yorkshire after Mickle Fell. The name gives a clue to its geology, because it derives from the Celtic *cweorn* or quern, side, meaning the hillside from where millstones were quarried. There are still arguments about the derivation of Pen-y-ghent's Celtic name, but the most popular appears to be the descriptive 'hill of the winds.' It suffers from the double misfortune of being on the Three Peaks route and having the Pennine Way cross its fine summit.

Ribblesdale, with the bustling market town of Settle at its foot, is a fine place to explore the geological skeleton of the Dales, and if you can't walk its fine hills, one of the best ways to see it is from the Settle–Carlisle railway line – 'the line that refused to die'.

This 72 mile (116km) route, one of the most scenic on the rail network, had been threatened with closure since the days of Dr Beeching. But a concerted and sustained campaign by local people and walkers who used the line to get to the heart of Ribblesdale, saved it. The 325 bridges, 21 viaducts, 14 tunnels and 21 stations are a great monument to Victorian confidence and to the 2,000 navvies and their families who built it between 1869–76. They lived under appalling conditions in a Western-style shanty town known as Batty Green at Ribblehead.

Their only other epitaph is in the tiny beech-shaded chapel of St Leonard's at Chapel-le-Dale, in the valley of the Chapel Beck between Ingleborough and Whernside, where 200 victims of a smallpox epidemic at Batty Green lie buried in the graveyard. A simple but moving tablet on the west wall of the chapel reads:

To the memory of those who through accidents lost their lives in constructing the railway works between Settle and Dent Head. This tablet was erected at the joint expense of their fellow workmen and the Midland Railway Company, 1869 to 1876.

A limestone pavement and a glacial erratic on Ingleborough, with Simon Fell in the distance
Left: The filigree arches of Batty Moss Viaduct at Ribblehead

57

'HILL OF THE WINDS'

On the slopes of Pen-y-ghent above Dale Head Farm

Although it is the lowest of the famed Three Peaks, Pen-y-ghent (the name is thought to mean hill of the winds) dominates Ribblesdale, and especially the 'capital' of Horton. Its 'lion couchant' profile is to my mind the finest hill shape in the Yorkshire Dales, and it acts as an irresistible magnet to the hillwalker. It has the double misfortune though of featuring both on the Three Peaks Walk and the Pennine Way and thus has been subject to serious erosion. I thought twice about including it in this selection, but its inescapable attraction and the success of the anti-erosion measures undertaken by the National Park authority finally convinced me.

From the car park in the centre of the village take the minor road right of the Parish Church of St Oswald. This passes the resurgence cave of Douk Ghyll away to the left and reaches the hamlet of Brackenbottom on the springline where the limestone begins (**1**). A gate (signposted) on the left leads you over a stile and on a clear track over Brackenbottom Scar.

Follow the path by the wall over little limestone scars until you reach the first of the anti-erosion measures mentioned earlier. The wooden duckboards look ugly and intrusive but they do transport the walker over the boggier sections of the track without widening it. You cross a ladder stile (**2**), with the noble, stepped profile of Pen-y-ghent ever beckoning ahead, before the final, steep pull up to the shoulder of the hill, when Fountains Fell (named after the abbey) appears ahead.

You have now joined the Pennine Way, so if you see some poor, overladen soul toiling up behind you, let him pass with your sincere condolences. The final ascent of Pen-y-ghent is actually quite an exciting scramble, as you have to pick your best way through the alternating outcrops of grit and limestone. Once on the gritstone cap of the mountain, the dreaded duckboards appear again winding away over more boggy bits to the white trig point by the wall which crosses the summit.

The views from Pen-y-ghent are among the finest to be seen in the Dales. Westwards across Ribblesdale, Ingleborough with Whernside behind, lord it, but the view to the east across Silverdale to Fountains Fell is wilder and more impressive, with the tiny isolated farms and the deepening chasm of Pen-y-ghent Gill attracting the eye.

Cross the wall by ladder stile and, ignoring the main track, take the footpath signed Foxup

Road (**3**). This follows the wall, at first descending northwards and then climbing over wet ground north-east towards Pen-y-ghent's quieter northern shoulder, Plover Hill.

The summits of Pen-y-ghent and Plover Hill – unlike those of Ingleborough and Whernside – are on the watershed of England, so streams feeding off to the east drain into the Wharfe and the North Sea and to the west, into the Ribble and the Irish Sea.

At the summit of windswept Plover Hill, cross a stile in the corner of the wall and follow the waymarks north, with fine views into Halton Gill and the forested ranks of Langstrothdale ahead. Down through a little band of gritstone, you descend to the watershed at the head of Foxup Moor (**4**), where you turn left on the bridleway which crosses Foxup and Horton Moor, via Swarth Gill Gate.

From the gate, follow the path alongside the wall to the south. Soon you will cross the well-trodden Three Peaks path (**5**), but turn sharply right heading north-west to reach Hull Pot Beck. Follow the beck downstream to reach the massive gaping rift of Hull Pot, where the stream plunges a giddying 60ft (18m) to disappear into the limestone. In times of flood, this huge chasm has actually been known to fill up with water.

The way back to Horton now follows the Pennine Way down the gentle undulations of walled Horton Scar Lane, with pleasant little outcrops of limestone lining and adding interest to the route.

FACT FILE

Map OS Outdoor Leisure Sheet 2, Yorkshire Dales (Western Area)
Start/Finish Horton-in-Ribblesdale car park, GR 808726
Length About 9 miles (14.5km)
Walking time Allow 4–5 hours
Difficulty A steep climb followed by boggy moorland and finishing on a walled lane

The Route in Brief

Start GR808726. From Horton take minor road R of church to Brackenbottom.
1 Take path L through gate (signposted Pen-y-ghent) across stile over Brackenbottom Scar.
2 Climb up to ladder stile and on up to shoulder of hill, where Pennine Way is joined from R. Turn L to scramble up to summit.
3 From summit, take path signed Foxup Road and follow wall descending N and then over Plover Hill. Follow waymarks N across stile.
4 Descend to head of Foxup Moor, where you turn L down via Swarth Gill Gate.
5 Cross Three Peaks track, and turn sharp R to Hull Pot Beck. Follow the beck downstream to Hull Pot. Then follow Pennine Way down Horton Scar Lane and back to Horton.

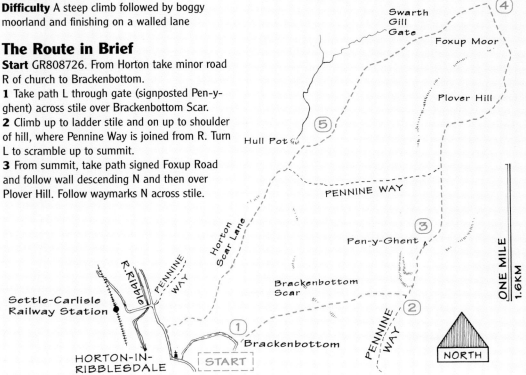

THE CAVES OF ATTERMIRE

For many visitors from the south, Settle is the gateway to the Dales – a busy little market town best avoided on Tuesdays when the square is filled with stalls. But many who use Settle as a base to explore the higher Three Peaks country miss the delights of the limestone country on Settle's back doorstep, in particular the caves and crags of Attermire which we visit on this easy afternoon stroll.

From the Market Square, walk up Constitution Hill (left of The Shambles) and when the road turns left, take the cobbled Banks Lane which branches steeply uphill to the right (**1**).

Beyond a small plantation at the top of Banks Lane, (**2**) turn right (signposted Malham) towards the prominent crags of Warrendale Knots and Attermire. This is one of the wildest and most interesting limestone landscapes in the Dales, a bit like Arizona with buttes and

Left: The caves and crags of Attermire
Opposite: The view from the inside of Victoria Cave, Attermire

FACT FILE

Map OS Outdoor Leisure Sheet 2, Yorkshire Dales (Western Area)

Start/Finish Settle GR 820637

Length 4 miles (6.5km)

Walking time Allow 2½ hours

Difficulty Easy walking after a steep start

The Route in Brief

Start GR 820637. Park in Market Square, Settle and walk up Constitution Hill.

1 Where road turns L, take R turn steeply up Banks Lane.

2 At top of lane, turn R (signposted Malham) towards Warrendale Knotts.

3 Follow path L and then N above a wall up to mouth of Victoria Cave.

4 Continue past Jubilee Caves, then descend to Langcliffe Lane, where a stile L leads across fields and through gates back to Banks Lane and Settle.

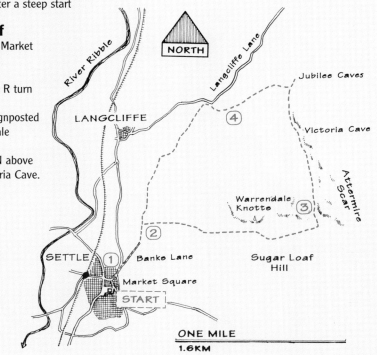

mesas of limestone soaring above deep and mysterious-looking caves – a wonderful place for children to explore.

The path turns left between Warrendale Knots and Attermire Scar with the slim vertical 'keyhole' of Attermire Cave high on the cliff face above the scree slopes ahead. It can be reached with care.

The path continues north above the wall along the foot of the scar, which towers above you to your right as you pass a series of caves. Many of these have given up secrets of their early occupation, the finds from which are displayed in Settle Museum. The most famous of these is Victoria Cave, named after the fact that it was discovered in 1838, the year of Queen Victoria's coronation.

The path climbs up to the impressive mouth of the cave (**3**), cleared to its present size by archaeologists. Care **must** be taken in its exploration because of recent rockfalls. Nearby are Wet Cave, the inevitable Albert Cave and Blackpot Cave, but all these should be left to experienced pot-holers.

Continue along to the twin Jubilee Caves before descending to the Langcliffe Lane. A stile on the left (**4**) leads below the Clay Pits Plantation and across the fields by a series of gates back to Banks Lane and down into Settle again.

THE WATERFALLS WALK

This is a walk guaranteed to cheer up the frustrated fellwalker stuck in the dales on days when the rain teems down and the 'clag' seems constantly to blanket the tops. For the Ingleton Glens walk actually *improves* after a period of heavy rain when the beautiful series of waterfalls in the twin ravines of the Twiss and Doe – surely the finest in the Dales – are in furious spate. The only disadvantage is that you have to pay for the privilege at the kiosk just off the car park under the disused railway viaduct which dominates the Ribblesdale village. Directions are hardly necessary for the walk, which throughout its length is on clear paths or along a quiet, drystone- walled lane.

The walk is usually done clockwise, and passing through the tree-shaded gorge of Swilla Glen, you eventually cross the Twiss at Twistleton Manor Bridge (**1**). Through a gate and you cross over again before reaching Pecca Falls, actually a series of three known as Pecca Twin Falls and Holly Bush Spout, deep in the trees but very impressive after rain.

Leaving the trees at Constitution Hill, the clear metalled path leads on past Cuckoo Island in the river, and the site of the old refreshment hut. At a sharp bend to the right, you get your first sight of the mightiest of the Ingleton waterfalls – Thornton Force. The Twiss thunders 45ft (14m) over a massive lip of limestone which projects over upturned beds of Precambrian slates in a superb natural amphitheatre. This is one of the classic sites in Dales geology. Take the rocky path which climbs steeply up left of the waterfall which deserts the river to wind around the grassy moraine hill of Raven Ray. Cross a footbridge to emerge on the quiet country byway of Twistleton Lane (**2**).

Turn right and follow the lane around the end of the rocky buttress of Twistleton Scar End, with superb views of flat-topped Ingleborough ahead. Past the farmhouse of Twistleton Hall you must cross Oddie's Lane and turn right (**3**) on the footpath which leads through Beezleys Farm and then descends into the twin valley of the River Doe.

The falls of the Doe – Beezley, Snow and Cat's Leap – are not as impressive as those of

The mighty Thornton Force

Map OS Outdoor Leisure Sheet 2, Yorkshire Dales (Western Area)
Start/Finish Ingleton Falls car park, GR 694733
Length About 4 miles (6.5km)
Walking time Allow 2½–3 hours
Difficulty Easy walking on graded paths, steps and a lane

The Route in Brief

Start GR 694733. From car park, ascend Swilla Glen by engineered pathway and steps.
1 Cross River Twiss at Twistleton Manor Bridge.
2 Past Thornton Force, climb steep path to L over Raven Ray and over footbridge to meet Twistleton Lane, where you turn R.
3 Past Twistleton Hall, cross Oddie's Lane and urn R to descend valley of River Doe back to Ingleton.

Ingleborough appears at the end of Twistleton Lane, near Beezleys Farm

the Twiss, and the lower part of the walk through Twistleton Glen is somewhat marred by the dusty and intrusive presence of Meal Bank Quarry over the river to the right.

Eventually you emerge in the centre of Ingleton close to the church and bus station. Turn right to return to the car park.

AN ERRATIC ROUTE

The barren, rocky area north of the pretty little Craven village of Austwick is one of the finest karst landscapes in Britain. Limestone lovers will delight in the outstanding clints and grikes, caves and scars of this dry, white land where the very skeleton of the landscape is exposed. Split by the green oasis of the valley of Crummackdale, this route also takes in a classic site in British geology – the Norber erratics.

The crag of Robin Proctor's Scar above Austwick from Wharfe Gill Sike

Austwick, mercifully by-passed by the A65, is a candidate for the prettiest village in the Dales, clustering around a tiny green and with field systems dating back to Celtic days. Park carefully in the village and take Townhead Lane to the north, and where it crosses Thwaite Lane (**1**), take the left-hand route and follow the sign (right) for Norber, crossing a stile.

The path wends up between limestone outcrops and onto the sloping Norber plateau, above Robin Proctor's Scar (apparently named after a farmer who jumped off it on his horse).

You will soon encounter the strange sight of the Norber erratics (**2**), large angular blocks of dark, lichened Silurian grit, some perched on plinths of limestone. These boulders were transported over half a mile by an Ice Age glacier from the western slopes of Crummackdale, where they outcrop naturally 400ft (122m) lower and *beneath* the limestone. Unequal weathering has left the boulders stranded as 'erratics'.

Return to the signpost and follow the footpath below Robin Proctor's Scar and across the field where the wall turns left back down to Thwaite Lane. Turn right and follow the lane

to its junction with Long Lane by the woods of Clapham Beck (**3**). Turn right here and follow the long, straight-walled track which runs parallel with Clapham Beck and below Thwaite Scars high to your right. Where the lane peters out into a green track, bear right (**4**) on a green track which leads on past Long Scar, with a splendid view ahead towards Pen-y-ghent.

You are now at the highest point of the walk on a green track between limestone outcrops. At the junction of walls at Sulber Gate (**5**), take the gate in the wall on the right and then the path which descends the evocatively named Thieves Moss, through strange outcrops and the edge of the natural amphitheatre which forms the head of Crummackdale. Dropping down to Beggar's Stile (**6**), a short detour along the edge of Moughton Scar, backed by the weird, white, rocky moonscape of Moughton, is well worthwhile. It is easy to see why this area, judging from place-names, was Ribblesdale's 'badlands' and the haunt of the local criminal fraternity.

Descend back down Crummackdale from Beggar's Stile. The route passes through a prehistoric settlement and past Austwick Beck Head Cave, where the waters of Austwick Beck emerge into view. Past Crummack Farm on the left, the route joins Crummack Lane (**7**), over Norber Brow and back down into Austwick.

A classic geological site: an erratic boulder at Norber with the scars of White Stone and Long Scar across Crummackdale beyond

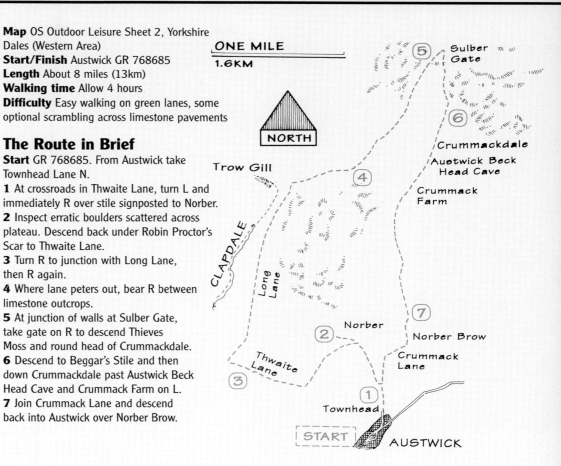

FACT FILE

Map OS Outdoor Leisure Sheet 2, Yorkshire Dales (Western Area)
Start/Finish Austwick GR 768685
Length About 8 miles (13km)
Walking time Allow 4 hours
Difficulty Easy walking on green lanes, some optional scrambling across limestone pavements

The Route in Brief
Start GR 768685. From Austwick take Townhead Lane N.
1 At crossroads in Thwaite Lane, turn L and immediately R over stile signposted to Norber.
2 Inspect erratic boulders scattered across plateau. Descend back under Robin Proctor's Scar to Thwaite Lane.
3 Turn R to junction with Long Lane, then R again.
4 Where lane peters out, bear R between limestone outcrops.
5 At junction of walls at Sulber Gate, take gate on R to descend Thieves Moss and round head of Crummackdale.
6 Descend to Beggar's Stile and then down Crummackdale past Austwick Beck Head Cave and Crummack Farm on L.
7 Join Crummack Lane and descend back into Austwick over Norber Brow.

ONE MILE
1.6KM

NORTH

Trow Gill
Sulber Gate
Crummackdale
Austwick Beck Head Cave
Crummack Farm
CLAPDALE
Long Lane
Norber
Norber Brow
Crummack Lane
Thwaite Lane
Townhead
START
AUSTWICK

POT LUCK ON A RIBBLE RAMBLE

Alum Pot Beck plunges into the cleft of Alum Pot

Although it doesn't attract the publicity of Gaping Gill which gapes spectacularly on Ingleborough's popular flanks, Alum Pot on lesser-known Borrins Moor is a pot-hole every bit as awesome. This easy, mostly level stroll takes in Alum Pot and passes a number of other caves and disappearing streams in a pleasant exploration of limestone country from Horton-in-Ribblesdale.

From the northern end of Horton, follow the Pennine Way signs into Harber Scar Lane (the old packhorse route to Hawes), to the right of The Crown Hotel. Ascend this rough track between the twin Sell Gill Holes, where Sell Gill Beck disappears underground into a chamber second only in size to Gaping Gill.

At a gate (**1**), leave the Pennine Way and follow the Birkwith signs left along a splendid level, green terrace between the limestone scars of High Pasture and Sheep Scar to the wooded ravine of Birkwith Gill. Beyond this, under the suitably named Dismal Hill, is the sinister black slit of Birkwith Cave.

Beyond Birkwith Gill, turn left (**2**) on the track down to High Birkwith, where you turn right (signed Selside) through Low Birkwith to cross the Ribble by a footbridge. A walled lane leads up under the Settle–Carlisle railway and crosses the road to Selside Farm (**3**) where you should call to pay the small charge required to visit Alum Pot, which is on private ground. Turn right up the road and take the first left to climb up to Alum Pot, embowered in trees and enclosed by a limestone wall.

This fearsome cleft is usually fed by the torrent of Alum Pot Beck, which falls a giddying 200ft (60m) into the inky depths and then cascades another 100ft (30m) before it reaches the bottom of the pot. Water from the Long Churn Pots and Diccan Cave on the hillside above also tumble into this impressive cauldron.

Having thoroughly (but carefully) explored this land of disappearing streams, retrace your steps but turn right as you reach the head of the walled lane (**4**). Just beyond Borrins Farm (**5**) turn right on a gently rising bridleway between limestone outcrops until you reach the Three Peaks track at Sulber Nick (**6**). Turn sharp left here to follow this well-beaten path through the limestone pavements and back into Horton, past the ugly man-made chasm and unnatural ultramarine ponds of Horton Quarry.

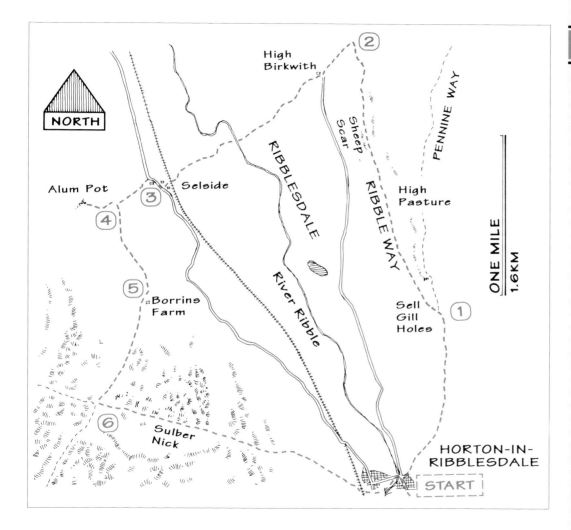

Map OS Outdoor Leisure Sheet 2, Yorkshire Dales (Western Area)
Start/Finish Horton-in-Ribblesdale car park GR 808726
Length About 10 miles (16km)
Walking time Allow 4–5 hours
Difficulty Easy, mostly level going over lanes and green pastures

The Route in Brief

Start GR 808726. Follow Pennine Way signs to Sell Gill Holes.
1 Follow signs L to Birkwith on green track between High Pasture and Sheep Scar.
2 Beyond Birkwith Gill turn L to High Birkwith then R under railway towards Selside.
3 At Selside Farm, turn R up road and first L to Alum Pot.
4 Retrace steps but turn R at head of lane.
5 Beyond Borrins Farm, turn R onto bridleway.
6 Turn sharp L on reaching Sulber Nick back to Horton.

THE CLAPHAM CLASSIC

The sainted Wainwright considered this way to the summit of Ingleborough the finest walk in the limestone country of the Dales, and I would not argue with his assessment. For continuous and varied interest along the way, a satisfying and fascinating summit which has its own story to tell, and a taste of all the geological wonders of the Dales, Ingleborough from Clapham is a classic.

Start in the National Park's Clapham car park, having first had a look in the information centre on the left. Turn right and then left over the packhorse bridge which crosses Clapham Beck. Turning right over the bridge, go up through the wood-yard of the Ingleborough Estate (1). A small charge is made to follow Clapdale Drive, an engineered path which 'winds' up through the woodlands planted by pioneer botanist Reginald Farrer, whose family seat was at nearby Ingleborough Hall. Alternatively, you can use the adjacent lane to the left, rejoining the route by a footpath beyond Clapdale Farm.

The paths emerge at the still waters of the lake which was constructed and used by the Farrer family to provide a water supply and electricity to Clapham as early as 1896. A fine example of the early use of a sustainable energy supply, the turbines are still in use today, providing electricity to the estate office and the adjoining house – and one street lamp.

Beyond the lake, you pass through a belt of native yew trees which thrive on the limestone soil and pass the ugly ornamental grotto constructed by Farrer on the left before passing through a gate and emerging from the woodland and into Clapdale proper. The path from Clapdale Farm joins here from the left, but you continue up the left bank of the beck, passing the thumping ram water-pump which feeds the farm above.

Now the limestone crags start to crowd in on either side and in a few steps you approach the impressive, overhung entrance to Ingleborough Cave (2), the oldest of the three major show-caves in the National Park. Just beyond the cave entrance is Beck Head, the equally impressive resurgence cave of Clapham Beck, which is known as Fell Beck before its headlong plunge into the depths of Gaping Gill a mile further on.

Now the dale narrows even more, and crossing a ladder stile (3), the path turns left into the gloomy confines of Trow Gill. Topped now by a filigree of pines, Trow Gill was formed by the tremendous power of glacial meltwater flowing down from the slopes of Ingleborough perhaps 10,000 years ago. An easy scramble and stile brings you out onto the open moorland known as Clapham Bottoms.

You are now on the moorland section of the walk and the going becomes rougher as you pass several sealed-off pot-holes such as Bar Pot on the left, all of which lead the caver into the grand-daddy of them all, Gaping Gill. This now appears in a crater-like depression in the moorland ahead (4). Admire its awesome gulf from a safe distance (it falls 340ft/104m sheer) before taking the clear but usually boggy path past Thack Pot and up onto the beckoning shoulder of Little Ingleborough.

Reaching the cairn at the ridge (5), turn right and follow the clear track which reaches the summit plateau of Ingleborough (2372ft/ 723m) at its south-east corner. The 15 acre (6ha) Iron Age hill fort which covers the summit is one of the biggest and certainly the highest in England, and may be the site known to the Romans as Rigodunum, the 'capital' of the rebel Brigantian leader, Venutious.

After admiring the extensive view from the summit shelter and exploring the insignificant remains of the 900m enclosing ramparts, retrace your steps down to Little Ingleborough. Bear right (almost due south) (6) here across Newby Moss and down the shallow, usually dry stream bed of Grey Wife Sike, which passes through a line of shake holes and grouse butts steadily down towards the hamlet of Newby Cote below.

Turn left here (7) onto the 'Old Road' between Clapham and Ingleton, a pleasant walled lane followed by the Yorkshire Dales Cycle Way which leads easily and quickly back into Clapham village.

The mouth of Gaping Gill, where Fell Beck drops 340ft (104m) sheer
Opposite: Entering the dry gorge of Trow Gill

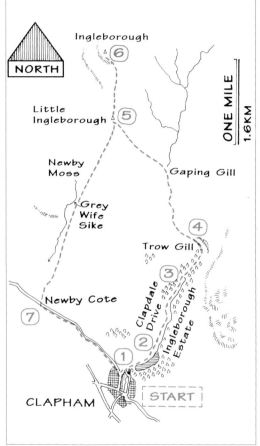

Whernside and the distant Howgills from Ingleborough's summit

FACT FILE

Map OS Outdoor Leisure Sheet 2, Yorkshire Dales (Western Area)
Start/Finish Clapham village car park GR 746692
Length About 9 miles (14.5km)
Walking time Allow at least 5 hours
Difficulty After easy woodland tracks, crosses high moorland with a steep climb to the summit. Good visibility recommended

The Route in Brief

Start GR 746692. From car park in turn R, crossing packhorse bridge L and then R again.
1 At Ingleborough Estate wood-yard, follow Clapdale Drive up through trees.
2 Continue through grounds of Ingleborough Estate to emerge in Clapdale and reach Ingleborough Cave.
3 Cross ladder stile L and enter Trow Gill. Climb out over stile.
4 Follow path across moorland to Gaping Gill and take boggy path L towards Little Ingleborough.
5 Climb up to ridge and turn R to climb gradually N to reach summit plateau of Inlgeborough.
6 Retrace steps to Little Ingleborough then bear R (S) across Newby Moss and down Grey Wife Sike to Newby Cote.
7 Turn L on walled lane leading back to Clapham.

DENTDALE AND GARSDALE: DALES APART

In the view of Mike Harding, entertainer, rambler and Dent resident, Dentdale is the loveliest of all the Yorkshire Dales. It is certainly different from all the rest. It has a softer, leafier aspect than the others and the fells seem to stand further back, as if making space to admire the sylvan scene beneath.

That abundance of trees and hedges is perhaps best appreciated when seen from the lower slopes of Whernside or from the ancient Galloway Gate drove road on the flanks of Great Knoutberry Fell at the eastern head of the dale. From here at around 1700ft (518m), you get a bird's-eye view down the broad, U-shaped dale, with the rounded shapes of the Howgills as a backdrop and the great whaleback of Whernside, with Ingleborough peeping over its shoulder, to the south.

Dentdale and its parallel neighbour Garsdale, wind west like the Ribble to eventually flow out into the Irish Sea, again in contradiction to the majority of Dales rivers, which head

Low Haygarth Fam, with the mile-long escarpment of Cautley Crag in the background

for the Humber and empty their waters into the grey North Sea.

The River Dee joins the Lune at the bustling little township of Sedbergh, lying in the seductive shadow of the smooth-sloped Howgill Fells. Sedbergh is famous for its boys' public school, and the school song pays tribute to the persuasive, 'character-forming' influence that the hills have had on pupils over the years, all of whom apparently have to climb Winder at least once in their school careers. 'It's Cautley, Calf and Winder, that make a Sedbergh man.'

In geological terms, the Howgills are a bit of an anomaly within the Yorkshire Dales National Park. They are an incredible 100 million years older than the Carboniferous rocks which make up the majority of the Dales, consisting of Silurian slates of the type found around Coniston in the southern Lake District. These 440 million-year-old rocks have weathered into the distinctive smooth, grassy slopes of the Howgills, which are so different from the steeply stepped, craggy profiles of the Yoredale series seen elsewhere in the Dales and at the eastern heads of Garsdale and Dentdale.

But the Howgills make fine walking country, and the ancient common grazing rights which exist on the fells mean that they are still to a large extent unfenced or walled, giving sweeping vistas and uninterrupted passage to the walker.

One word of warning, though. In mist or fog, it is notoriously easy to get lost on the Howgills, and a map and compass are **essential** for safe progress under these conditions. As stated above, there are very few crags in the Howgills, but the deep gashes of gorges like Cautley Spout, The Spout or Black Force and the impressive mile-long line of Cautley Crags leading north to the celebrated waterfall are definitely *not* places you want to stumble over in mist.

I well remember the day when, traversing the Howgills from the valley of Chapel Beck, we approached the highest point of The Calf (2219ft/676m). Suddenly and without warning we were enveloped by a clinging, swirling mist which appeared from nowhere. Only a compass bearing told us the way forward to Bram Rigg Top, Arant Haw and Winder and eventually down to Sedbergh.

A favourite walk from 'Dent Town', as the

tiny village at the hub of the dale is incongruously known, is over Whernside via what local people know as 'the Ocky'. The full name for this ancient, walled green lane is the Occupation Road, recalling the time when the moorland was being reclaimed, or 'occupied', for the first time. This track leads all the way from the sequestered, perfect little glaciated dale of Barbondale, which leads south-west to Kirkby Lonsdale, around the flanks of Great Coum and Deepdale to drop down into the Viking valley of Kingsdale.

Dent's cobbled main street is punctuated by a huge monolith of Shap granite which forms a simple yet moving memorial to Dent's most famous son. Adam Sedgwick was born in 1785, the son of the local vicar. He went to Sedbergh School, where he undoubtedly fell under the influence of the Howgill Fells and the strange local sequence of rocks caused by faults in the Earth's crust. After a distinguished academic career which took him to Cambridge University, Sedgwick became a professor and one of the founding fathers of the modern science of geology. Among his more important work was the discovery and explanation of his local and now celebrated Dent Fault.

'Unconformities' – as such a sequence of rocks out of chronological order is known – seem to be a speciality of Dentdale. About 2 miles (3.2km) west of Sedbergh on the Kendal road stands a small, neat whitewashed building with a solid stone porch, known as Brigflatts, which was the first nonconformist Quaker meeting house in the country.

Here in 1675, the earliest Friends' Meeting House was established, probably under the influence of George Fox, the founder of this pacifist movement, who was a regular preacher in these parts. He once spoke to a crowd of thousands at a place still known as Fox's Pupil, on the slopes of Firbank Fell, just across the Lune Gorge, which enjoys an unequalled and no doubt inspiring view of the folded western flanks of the Howgills as a backdrop.

Another famous Dalesman Quaker, the historian and geologist Dr Arthur Raistrick, dubbed Dentdale and Garsdale 'the remote dales', and they are still some way off the usual tourist itinerary. Perhaps it is because they do not have the spectacular beauty spots of the better-known dales like Wensleydale and Wharfedale. But to those who have explored their subtle charms and well-kept secrets, these 'dales apart' are every bit as rewarding as their more famous counterparts. The most important industry is still stock farming, the one which brought the original Norse settlers here. And in some ways, they show the discerning visitor what the Dales used to be like, before tourism took the inevitable hold it has elsewhere in the area.

FOLLOWING THE DROVERS

The Settle and Carlisle Railway was a triumph of optimism over adversity. The 72 mile (116km) route through some of the most difficult country in Britain was the epitome of Victorian engineering confidence, and the storm of protest which arose when it was proposed for closure in the 1980s showed the special place it holds in the national affection.

Thankfully now saved, the S&C is a great asset to the Yorkshire Dales and the recent move by the National Park to make its entire length a Conservation Area should give it welcome extra protection. The spectacular line makes an ideal vehicle for linear walks in the Dales with the added bonus that by using it, you will be helping to safeguard its future. I did the following walk while staying at Appleby, reaching the starting and finishing point by the S&C.

Dent Station, like many of those on the S&C, is many a mile from the village which it serves, and at an altitude of 1150ft (350m) above the sea, one of the highest in Britain. It gives a good start to this walk which wends around the head of Dentdale.

Turn right out of the station and take the steep lane known as the Coal Road, past the plantation of Dodderham Moss on the left to its junction with Galloway Gate (**1**), the signposted bridleway on the right. This ancient drovers' road is thought to get its name from the fact that Scottish-bred cattle were driven down it to the markets of industrial England.

Galloway Gate contours gently around the slopes of Great Knoutberry Hill, giving grand, panoramic views down the length of Dentdale leading off west to the distant Howgills, and with Whernside, Gragareth and Ingleborough to the south.

Passing a series of swallow and shake holes and disused coal pits, turn sharply right downhill (**2**) and onto the rough track which leads down Arten Gill. Before long, the lace-like frieze of Artengill Viaduct – one of twenty-one on the route – appears crossing the beck ahead. Pass beneath it to cross the River Dee and turn right (**3**) to join the minor road (followed by the Dales Way) which accompanies the river back down into the dale.

Turn right after about half a mile at Lea Yeat (**4**), crossing the river again and then up quite steeply for another half mile, up Helmsike Hill to arrive back at Dent Station and your starting point.

Dent Station, the starting point of this walk, is one of the highest in Britain at 1150ft (350m)

Walkers ascend the track beneath the Artengill Viaduct, which carries the Settle–Carlisle Railway

Note: This walk could be started at Garsdale Station (GR 788917), following the metalled section of Galloway Lane across Garsdale Common and Windy Hill, to join this route at the top of the Coal Road.

FACT FILE

Map OS Outdoor Leisure Sheet 2, Yorkshire Dales (Western Area)
Start/Finish Dent Station GR 764875
Length About 5 miles (8km)
Walking time Allow 3 hours

Difficulty Some roadwork and steep hills, but nothing too tough

The Route in Brief
Start GR 764875. Turn R from station and uphill on Coal Road.

1 At top, turn L onto Galloway Gate drove road.

2 After about 2 miles (3.2km), turn sharp R downhill to join track down Arten Gill.

3 Under Artengill Viaduct, cross River Dee and turn R on minor road.

4 After about ½ mile (0.8km), turn R at road junction up Helmsike Hill and back to Dent Station.

ONE MILE
1.6KM

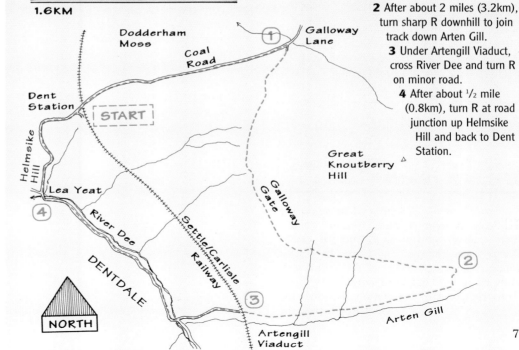

79

ON 'THE OCKY'

Marked on the map as 'Green Lane (Track)', the ancient walled track which skirts Great Coum and Crag Hill above the little township of Dent is known locally as 'the Ocky'. The abbreviation is short for the Occupation Road, and it marks the upper limit of the enclosure or 'occupation' of the fellside in the mid-1800s. It also follows the line of the Ingleton to Lancaster packhorse trail, which was formerly a major commercial route across the Dales.

This route follows the best section of 'the Ocky' for views across Dentdale to the distant Howgills and descends back into the dale for some pleasant walking along the dale bottom. Start by crossing the road from the large car park in Dent and take the lane by the Memorial Hall which soon turns into a stony track on the right bank of wooded Flinter Gill.

At the top, with fine views across to the Howgills, turn right (**1**) and along the wide green lane of the Occupation Road as it winds around the lower slopes of Great Coum and Crag Hill. Now go down across South Lord's Land to the Barbondale Road,

with the expanse of Middleton Fell ahead.

Turn right here (**2**) and then left through a gate where a footpath leads off across Stone Rigg below Combe (or Dent) Scar to the ruins of Combe House. Combe Scar marks the Dent fault and is composed of dark Silurian grits. The path leads on down to Tofts, another ruin, where the beck is crossed by a stone-slab clapper bridge. Up the opposite bank, the route gradually drops down Bower Bank to join a lane at Underbank (**3**).

Turn right and drop down to the pleasant lit-tle village of Gawthrop, whose Norse name is said to mean the village of the crows. Cross Oliver Gill by the bridge and take the track on the right past a phone box (**4**), crossing another beck and forking right and through the fields across Doblin's Hill and Mill Beck Hill to drop down into the hamlet of Mill Beck.

Keep to the track through Mill Beck and descend through the fields and a caravan and camping site to rejoin the road next to the Methodist Chapel in Dent. Turn right to get back to the centre of the village.

From the churchyard in Dent
Left: On the 'Ocky' – the occupation road – looking towards the northern wall of Dentdale

Map OS Outdoor Leisure Sheet 2, Yorkshire Dales (Western Area)
Start/Finish Dent GR 704871
Length About 5 miles (8km)
Walking time Allow 3–4 hours
Difficulty Moderate walking along a green lane, then across enclosed fields

The Route in Brief

Start GR 704871. From car park take the lane up Flinter Gill.

1 At the top, turn R and along the Occupation Road and down to the Barbondale Road.

2 Turn R and then L beneath Combe Scar, crossing beck near Tofts.

3 Descend Bower Bank to join lane at Underbank. Turn R into Gawthrop.

4 Cross bridge and turn R past phone box then across fields to Mill Beck and back to Dent.

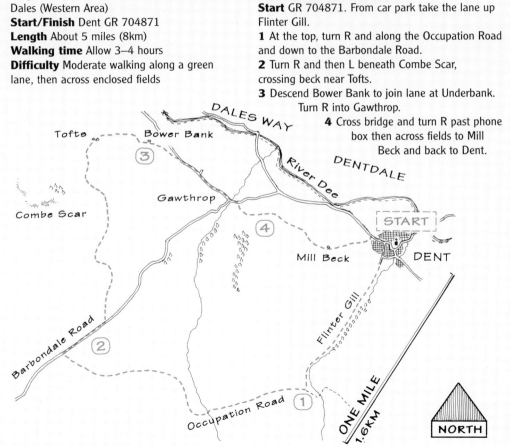

HIGHLIGHTS OF THE HOWGILLS

The cascades of Cautley Spout

The two most spectacular scenic highlights of the seductively smooth Howgill Fells are visited in this varied walk to their highest point – The Calf. The 6 mile (10km) walk involves some steep scrambling in its early sections beside the 700ft (213m) waterfalls of Cautley Spout, but for my money it is the classic half-day excursion into the innermost heart of the Howgills.

Start from the generous parking space provided to the east of the Cross Keys Temperance Hotel, where an inscription carved over a doorway quotes William Blake:

Great things are done when men and mountains meet;
This is not done by jostling in the street.

Fortified by that rather sexist exhortation, drop down to the pleasant little footbridge which crosses the River Rawthey and turn left up the muddy farm track which skirts the Scottish-sounding Ben End before joining another track leading up from the ford which serves Low Haygarth Farm (**1**). Rounding Ben End, you start to climb gently on a grassy track through bracken, crossing streams into the grand valley of Cautley Holme Beck.

Now the scenery starts to improve with every step, with the mile-long shattered cliff of Cautley Crag revealing itself in all its savage glory across the beck to the left, and the silver ribbon of Cautley Spout dancing in its wooded cleft ahead. This is one of the finest views in the Howgills.

The path now starts to climb steeply, heading directly towards the now clearly audible Lower Falls of Cautley. It was here, many years ago, that I met by chance that doyen of fellwanderers, Alfred Wainwright, who described this place as 'the most impressive corner of the Howgills'.

The next section of the route is the most difficult as you ascend steeply (**2**) on a badly eroded path which skirts the awesome waterfall to your left. Hung over by clinging rowans and dripping mosses, the falls drop in a series of graceful dives into pools deep beneath your feet. **Take care**, because a slip could be fatal.

Still climbing, the path wends around some weathered Silurian crags, while the breathtaking view behind now extends down the full length of the meandering Cautley Holme Beck towards the bulk of Baugh Fell to the south-east.

The Upper Falls of Cautley are possibly even more beautiful that the lower, cascading in a delicate fan over moss-covered rock. Now you must contour into the upper level of the gorge, crossing the waters of Swere Gill (3) which enter from the right.

At last the gradient eases and you emerge from the clamour of the gorge into the strangely silent upland valley of Force Gill Beck. The path, indistinct at times, winds up the left bank of the beck to the head of the valley, and the col between The Calf to your right and Bram Rigg Top to your left.

Turn right at the top of the grassy staircase to the col (4) and climb gently up the broad track to the 2219ft/676m summit of The Calf, with its fine views of the Lakeland skyline across the Eden Valley to the north-east and towards Three Peak Country to the south-east.

After a well-earned rest, retrace your steps down to the col and follow the Sedbergh track which crosses Bram Rigg Top and on to Calders. Turn left here (5) and follow the fence (one of the few anywhere on the usually unenclosed Howgills) down to where it turns sharply to the right. Set off across the broad, heathery top of Great Dummacks above Coonthard Brow to the edge of the impressive precipice of Cautley Crag, leading the eye to the ribbon of Cautley Spout and the noble summit of Yarlside to the right.

Now follow the grassy slopes to the left of Pickering Gill down to the footbridge crossing Cautley Holme Beck near a barn, and retrace your steps back to the Rawthey footbridge.

FACT FILE

Map OS Outdoor Leisure Sheet 19, Howgill Fells and Upper Eden
Start/Finish Cross Keys Inn, Cautley, GR 698969
Length About 6 miles (10km)
Walking time Allow 4 hours
Difficulty The first part of the walk is quite strenuous, and once on the tops, navigation could be difficult in mist

The Route in Brief
Start GR 698969. Descend to footbridge across the Rawthey and turn L along track.

1 Join track from Low Haygarth and turn right into valley of Cautley Holme Beck.
2 Climb steeply up path by Lower and Upper waterfalls of Cautley Spout.
3 Cross Swere Gill and enter upper valley of Force Gill Beck. Climb easily up to col.
4 Here turn R to summit of The Calf. Retrace your steps to col.
5 Walk up to cross Bram Rigg Top and Calders, where you turn L and follow fence until it turns R. Then head across Great Dummacks and down to L of Pickering Gill to cross Cautley Holme Beck and return by your outward route.

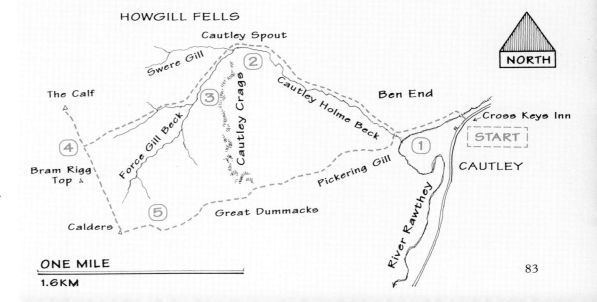

ONE MILE

1.6KM

PLACE OF THE WILD BOARS

Strictly speaking, this walk is outside the bounds of the Yorkshire Dales National Park, but the wild valley of Mallerstang and Wild Boar Fell is a wilderness experience not to be missed.

Passengers on the infamous 'Long Drag' between Kirkby Stephen and Ais Gill summit – the highest point on the Settle and Carlisle railway – get a glimpse of these grim heights beetling above them. But only the walker can really get to know the fell tops, where reputedly the last wild boar in England was killed.

The walk starts from the disused quarry beside the B5269 Moorcock–Kirkby Stephen road which threads through Mallerstang. Turn left out of the quarry and walk down the road across the bridge which is a favourite vantage point for train-spotters watching steam 'specials' on the S&C.

When Aisgill Farm appears surrounded by trees to the right, turn left (**1**) on a farm track which leads uphill to the left and under the Ais Gill railway viaduct.

The tracks of the Settle–Carlisle railway at Ais Gill Summit, the highest point of the line

The track leads to the tree-shaded limestone gorges of Ais Gill, known as Low White and White Kirk, down to the left. Bear off right here (**2**) across the moor, keeping the intake wall on your right. Where it bends away towards the valley bottom, head north past the series of open pot-holes known as Angerholme Pots, on the junction of the limestone and gritstone. Climb gradually up to the end of the escarpment of Wild Boar Fell, which is known by the delightful name of Scriddles.

At the ridge top (**3**), turn left along the crest of the escarpment to the prominent crags of The Nab, which have been watching your progress past the Angerholme Pots below. The next top of Blackbed Scar has a series of fine cairns, and from here, if you plan to 'bag' the 2324ft/708m summit of Wild Boar Fell, you must turn due west, where the trig point beckons sheltered by a decrepit stone wall.

Tucked in below the summit to the west are the waters of Sand Tarn, a delightful and secluded mountain lake, the gritty sands of which Wainwright claimed were once used for sharpening scythes and where millstones were quarried from the boulder slopes above. Certainly, like many Dales landscapes, Wild Boar Fell has seen its share of industry, with the remains of peat cutting, lead mines, millstone quarries and lime kilns scattered across its now-deserted flanks.

From the summit, turn south-west and then south to the col (4) between Wild Boar Fell and Swarth Fell, where another little unnamed tarn is encountered. Ascend by the wall which marks the county boundary between North Yorkshire and Cumbria to the summit of Swarth Fell (2234ft/681m).

From Swarth Fell Pike, turn left (5) and descend the open moor heading towards the left bank of Far Cote Gill, which will return you to Cotegill Bridge and the quarry where you left your car.

Walkers descend the north ridge of Wild Boar Fell

Map OS Outdoor Leisure Sheet 19, Howgill Fells and Upper Eden Valley
Start/Finish On road opposite Cotegill Bridge Quarry, GR 774969
Length About 7 miles (11km)
Walking time Allow 4 hours
Difficulty Serious fell walking and steep ascents

The Route in Brief

Start GR 774969. Turn L and walk down road to Aisgill Farm (R).
1 Turn L under railway viaduct to Ais Gill gorge.
2 Bear R across moor by wall, then L past Angerholme Pots to escarpment end.
3 At top of ridge, turn L to ascend Nab and then R to Wild Boar Fell summit.
4 Head SW to col between Wild Boar Fell and Swarth Fell. Ascend Swarth Fell by wall.
5 At Swarth Fell Pike, turn L to descend across moor via Far Cote Gill to return to quarry.

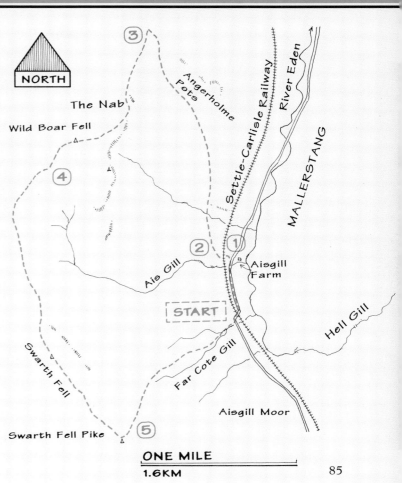

NORTH

The Nab
Wild Boar Fell
Angerholme Pots
Settle-Carlisle Railway
River Eden
MALLERSTANG
Ais Gill
Aisgill Farm
START
Swarth Fell
Far Cote Gill
Hell Gill
Aisgill Moor
Swarth Fell Pike

ONE MILE
1.6KM

6

WENSLEYDALE: A DALE OF SURPRISES

Although it may not have the overall grandeur of Wharfedale or the stern, northern wildness of Swaledale, Wensleydale is perhaps the most typical of all the Yorkshire Dales.

It is broad and expansive, well-settled with a string of beautiful stone-built villages clustering around their greens such as West Burton, Askrigg and Bainbridge, and it is rich in historical interest. Its many side-dales such as Coverdale, Waldendale, Bishopdale and Widdale, are relatively unfrequented and reward diligent exploration. Walkers will soon discover that what Wensleydale may lack in spectacular landscapes, it more than makes up for in its little gems of scenic beauty and places of indi-vidual interest.

Authorities as diverse as John Wesley and Charles Kingsley rated Wensleydale as the most beautiful of all the Dales, and even the moorland tramper Alfred Brown conceded that it was the most representative, serving as a 'useful introduction' to the other dales of the west.

A frosty morning on Askrigg, looking across the dale towards Crag Fell (left) and Wether Fell

One of Wensleydale's major attractions is its fine collection of waterfalls, formed after glaciation had smoothed the valley floor and the resultant rivers and becks had worn away the softer shales between harder steps of limestone. Wensleydale's watery wonderlands range from the awesome 90ft (27m) plunge of Hardraw Force, near Hawes, to the spectacular series of three which fall about 200ft (60m) in half a mile at Aysgarth.

One other watery oddity, not strictly in Wensleydale but in the adjoining valley of Raydale, is the 90 acre (36ha) Semer Water, the largest, and (with Malham Tarn) the only sizeable natural lake in the National Park.

Lying in a hollow formed by Ice Age glaciers, Semer Water is a reminder of what many of the dales would have looked like soon after the passing of the glaciers. Once much larger than it is now, it was formed by glacial meltwater being impounded by a bank of moraine. The Carlow Stone and the Mermaid Stones, grey-black boulders found at the edge of the lake, are glacial erratics of Shap granite left behind by the retreating ice.

Every Dales child knows the legend of Semer Water; how an angel was refused shelter anywhere in the dale except at a shepherd's shieling high on the fells, and how the next morning the angelic curse drowned the dale:

Semerwater rise; Semerwater sink:
And swallow all the town, save this li'le house
Where they gave me meat and drink.

As is often the case with folklore, there may be some truth in the story because the remains of a prehistoric lake dwelling, or crannog, have been found beneath Semer Water. The insistence of local people that they could see the roofs of a submerged city beneath the still waters are, however, much harder to substantiate.

The modern 'capital' of Wensleydale is Hawes, a bustling little upland township which took over the unofficial title from Askrigg at the end of the seventeenth century, when it was granted its surprisingly late market charter.

Visit Hawes on a Tuesday and you will encounter real dalespeople about their essential business of buying or selling stock at the market. But like most country markets, that at Hawes is as much a social occasion as a business one. Much chewing of the fat is done among these

hardened hill people for whom this is often the only time they will see their neighbours from week to week, even those at the next farm.

Hawes, with its excellent National Park Visitor Centre and Museum of Dales Life at the old railway station, is also the home of one of the most famous gastronomic delicacies of the Dales – Wensleydale cheese. Probably first made from ewe's milk by the monks of Jervaulx Abbey, the creamy, crumbly Wensleydale cheese is still made from local milk at Hawes Creamery, once threatened but now thankfully saved by local enterprise.

Just across the dale from Hawes is the spectacular waterfall of Hardraw Force, behind the Green Dragon Inn in the little hamlet of Hardraw. This is one Dales scene you should not miss, as the waters of Fossdale Gill tumble over the lip of the overhanging natural amphitheatre of Hardraw Scaur in a solid column of dancing spray. It is doubly impressive in winter when the sweeping bedding planes of overhanging limestone are festooned by scintillating chandeliers of ice.

Aysgarth Falls are lower down the dale near its junction with Bishopsdale, and the Upper, Middle and Lower Falls are a popular attraction,

Left: Wild Boar Fell from the ancient road known as the High Way
Right: This late seventeenth-century farmhouse at Worton is a good example of Dales' vernacular architecture

with viewing platforms and an interpretive centre provided for visitors. A pleasant stroll can be taken through the leafy glades of Freeholders' Wood, where the National Park authority has undertaken a coppicing programme.

Among the many man-made attractions of Wensleydale, the perfect little medieval township of Middleham which guards the entrance to the dale, stands out. Clustered around the imposing ruin of Middleham Castle, stronghold of the Nevilles and once the home of Richard, Duke of Gloucester, it was known as 'the Windsor of the North' and retains an air of feudal superiority, perhaps emphasised by the racehorses still bred there.

Further up the dale guarding the entrance to Apedale is Castle Bolton, another four-square structure, but this time built by the de Scrope family in the fourteenth century as much as a palace as a castle. Among earlier distinguished, if unwilling, visitors was the ill-fated Mary, Queen of Scots.

The de Scropes had earlier given some of their extensive Wensleydale estates to the Cistercian monks of Jervaulx Abbey, near Masham, where the dale opens out onto the Plain of York. These romantic ruins, now filled with wild flowers and herbs, remind us again on what the wealth of the dale was founded. Not only is this the area where the first Wensleydale cheese was made, it was also produced two important breeds of sheep – the popular crossbred Masham and the curly fleeced Wensleydale. Nowhere was the term 'golden fleece' more appropriate.

AYSGARTH FALLS AND CASTLE BOLTON

The stepped cascade of the Lower Falls at Aysgarth

John Ruskin described Aysgarth Falls as '... out and out the finest thing in water I've seen in these islands', and the series of three spectacular waterfalls taken by the River Ure is certainly one of the finest sights in the Dales.

The falls were formed as a result of the Ure undercutting softer shale beds between harder beds of limestone, creating the terraced appearance. The circular pot-holes seen in the flatter areas of limestone were created when small pebbles were swirled around in hollows when the river was in flood.

Freeholders' Wood, through which the Middle and Lower Falls are reached, is a nature reserve which is being sensitively managed by traditional coppicing methods by the National Park authority. It gets its name from the fact that local people still hold commoners' rights to use it.

This easy 6 mile (10km) stroll combines the falls at Aysgarth with a visit to one of the finest fortified medieval manor houses in England. It heads north to the semi-feudal village of Castle Bolton, dominated by the fortified manor of the de Scropes, and returns via the quaint Quaker village of Carperby.

From the National Park car park and Visitor Centre at Aysgarth Falls, follow the signs down on engineered paths to the waterfalls, each of which are provided with viewing platforms. After admiring the falls, return through Freeholders' Wood to the Lower Force (**1**) where a signpost to Castle Bolton leads left across the fields to Hollins House Farm. Passing to the right of the farm, bear right with a fence on your right. On reaching a wall, turn right over a stile and continue across the next field towards a group of farm buildings.

Bear right over another stile and through a gap in a wall to eventually reach the hedged green track of Thoresby Lane (**2**), which leads to Low Thoresby Farm, occupying the site of a deserted medieval village.

Beyond the farm, bear left over a footbridge, turning left through a gap in a fence. Ignore the ladder stile in front and turn right across a field towards a barn. Passing to the right of the barn, cross another field to emerge onto a lane (**3**) which leads down to Castle Bolton village.

Castle Bolton is a one-street village of cottages clustered around a wide green and nestling beneath the protective walls of the castle. Privately-owned Bolton Castle was built by Sir Richard de Scrope in 1378 as a fortified manor house, and it is well worth a visit, if only for the fine views of Wensleydale which can be enjoyed from its walls. Mary, Queen of Scots was an enforced guest here for nearly a year.

Continue by taking the lane which leads past the castle and its car park. Over a stile, bear left (**4**) and follow the waymarked route through

The massive south-east tower of Bolton Castle

Map OS Outdoor Leisure Sheet 30, Yorkshire Dales (Northern and Central Areas)
Start/Finish Aysgarth Falls car park, GR 012887
Length 6 miles (10km)
Walking time Allow 4 hours
Difficulty Easy riverside and field paths

The Route in Brief

Start GR 012887. From NP Visitor Centre walk down to explore falls.
1 From the Lower Force, take path signed Castle Bolton through fields and round Hollins House Farm.
2 Follow Thoresby Lane to Low Thoresby Farm, bearing L over footbridge then R towards a barn.
3 Reaching a lane, descend into Castle Bolton village.
4 Walk past the castle and over a stile, bear L following waymarks into wooded Beldon Beck.
5 Passing L of West Bolton Farm cross a stream and turn R into Carperby.
6 Opposite the Wheatsheaf pub, turn L crossing Low Lane and bearing L back to Freeholders' Wood and Aysgarth.

the fields into the wooded valley of Beldon Beck, which is crossed by a footbridge.

The path then passes to the left of West Bolton Farm, and then to the north of West Bolton Plantation. Crossing a stream, you descend across the fields to East End Farm, turning right (**5**) on reaching the lane to the village of Carperby.

Carperby was given market rights in 1303 and later became an important centre of the Quaker movement. Opposite the Wheatsheaf pub, turn left (**6**) through a gate and follow the path through the fields, to cross Low Lane. Bear left to eventually re-enter Freeholders' Wood, turning left under the former railway bridge to return to the car park at Aysgarth.

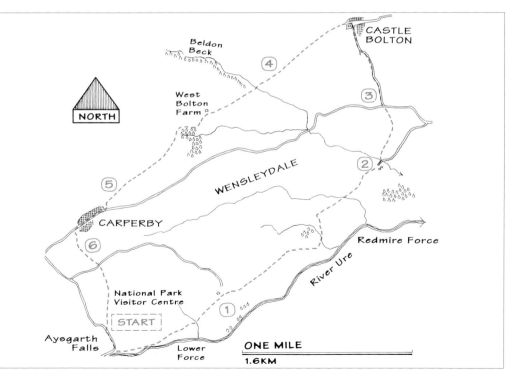

PIKE HILL AND HARDRAW FORCE

Pike Hill, at 1750ft (533m), is merely a southern shoulder of the main summit of Lovely Seat (2215ft/675m) which dominates the Buttertubs Pass between Wensleydale and Swaledale. But despite its appealing title and subsidiary features with equally charming names such as Lovely Seat End, Lover Gill and Lover Gill Head, Lovely Seat is anything but romantic. It is a featureless, boggy fell which on close acquaintance has limited views and little else but its altitude to commend it. Not so little Pike Hill and its bold southern escarpment of High Clint, which lords it over the head of Wensleydale and the charming little market town of Hawes, offering superb views of Widdale down to Ingleborough and into Garsdale. Linked to one of Wensleydale's great 'sights' – England's highest above-ground waterfall at Hardraw – this easy 7 mile (11km) walk more than repays the effort.

Starting from the centre of Hawes – busy market town for upper Wensleydale – take Brunt Acres Road north to Haylands Bridge across the Ure, where you turn left across a stile (**1**) and over the fields to the quiet hamlet of Sedbusk, crossing the road which leads down the dale to Askrigg.

Walk up through the cottages of Sedbusk on walled Shutt Lane (**2**) and at a gate at the end, turn left across a stile (**3**). This track leads up through limestone pastures with extensive views across the crags of High Clint ahead, to Wether Fell, Dodd Fell and Widdale Fell across the dale.

Near a limekiln, the path winds right through High Pasture Gate and up onto the plateau above the crags of Low Clint. It is now a short step to the summit, where a series of prominent cairns (or 'stone men') add foreground interest to the stupendous views which extend as far as Ingleborough and Whernside to the south.

The 100ft (30m) free drop of Hardraw Force is one of the scenic showplaces of the Dales

FACT FILE

Map OS Outdoor Leisure Sheet 30, Yorkshire Dales (Northern and Central Areas)
Start/Finish Hawes GR 876899
Length About 7 miles (11km)
Walking time Allow 3–4 hours
Difficulty Mostly across easy limestone pastures, with some lane walking

The Route in Brief

Start GR 876899, from Hawes, taking Brunt Acres Road leading N to Haylands Bridge across the Ure.
1 Take the stile (R) which leads to field paths to Sedbusk, crossing the lane to Askrigg.
2 Walk up through Sedbusk and take the walled track (Shutt Lane) which leads up the hill out of the hamlet.
3 Take the stile on the L, where a track leads across the fields heading towards the eastern end of Low Clint. The path swings round the crags (R) and then up onto the summit.
4 From here follow the obvious path leading N to Shivery Gill. Cross the gill and turn L down to the Buttertubs Pass road, where you turn L again to descend the lane for about 1½ miles (2.5km) to High Shaw.
5 Turn R into Foss Dale, passing a series of falls, then back to West House Farm for a visit to Hardraw Force.
6 Follow the Pennine Way across fields back to Haylands Bridge, turning R back into Hawes.

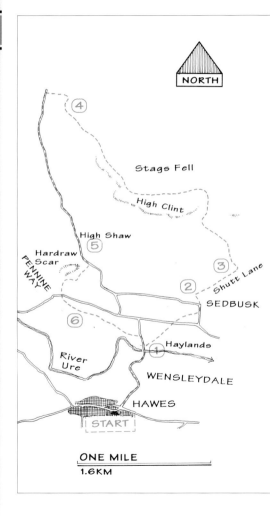

Walk north along the plateau edge, enjoying this splendid panorama to reach Pike Hill summit and its fine collection of beacons, and the view up the Buttertubs to its twin sentinels of Great Shunner Fell and Lovely Seat. Now drop down to the road after crossing the well-named Shivery Gill, and turn left (**4**), dropping down for about 1½ miles (2.5km) to reach High Shaw.

Turn right here (**5**) on a lane signposted Foss Dale, dropping down some steps through the trees and passing a series of waterfalls before returning to the road and back via West House Farm to the Green Dragon at Hardraw, where you must pay a small fee to see Hardraw Force in its impressive scaur.

In this impressive amphitheatre, Fossdale Gill plunges unbroken for 100ft (30m) in a column of dancing spray. It is especially dramatic in winter, when icicles form into great scintillating swords and daggers hanging from the dark rocks. Just downstream from the fall, a circular enclosure is still sometimes used for summer-time brass band contests in this natural theatre.

From Hardraw, cross the road to take the causey-flagged Pennine Way (**6**) by the bridge back across the fields to Haylands Bridge, turning right to Hawes, which is about a mile (1.6km) away.

THE CIRCUIT OF ADDLEBROUGH

Seen from the shores of Semer Water or from Bainbridge, the mighty prow of Addlebrough (1564ft/476m) can look more than a little like Conan Doyle's Lost World. Rising proudly from the green pastures of Wensleydale, enmeshed in their network of drystone walls and barns, the great plateau-like summit looks remote enough to be inhabited by the pterodactyls and other Palaeozoic monsters encountered by Professor Challenger and his gallant band of explorers.

Unfortunately for the walker, Addlebrough is almost as inaccessible as Mount Roraima in far-off Guyana, for no rights-of-way cross its flat-topped summit. This is a great pity, because Addlebrough commands spectacular views up and down Wensleydale and was the site of one of Venutious's Brigantian hill forts. An ancient cairn on its northern crest probably marks the burial place of the British chieftain called Authulf, who gave the hill its name, and below the summit to the south and west are extensive hut circles and settlements dating from the Bronze Age.

Right: Addlebrough as seen from Askrigg on the north bank of the Ure

Our circuit of this outstanding landmark starts from the little hamlet of Worton, just east of Bainbridge. Take the lane which leads steeply up to the south to the neighbouring hamlet of Cubeck. Turn right then left (**1**) up another steeply rising walled track to get your first view of Addlebrough, rising impressively ahead. This path contours around the northern slopes of the hill, just below a line of shake holes, where streams dip underground as they hit the limestone.

After about a mile (1.6km), the path reaches the cul-de-sac lane to Carpley Green, and you turn left (**2**) walking along the lane for about a mile (1.6km) towards the isolated farmstead. There are good views across to the crags of Addlebrough, including the prominent Devil's Stone, to your left, and the remains of one of the prehistoric settlements may be picked out just beneath the escarpment.

Just before reaching Carpley Green, turn left through a gate (**3**), and follow the path which leads parallel to and above a wall on your right. By ascending the slopes to your left towards the summit (no right-of-way), you get a fine aerial view of Semer Water to the west. There are other prehistoric settlements on Stony Raise on the slopes of Greenber opposite.

The path now crosses the featureless expanse

of Thornton Rust Moor (4), before dropping down through another line of shake holes to a walled track which leads down into the village.

Turn left along the lane and to the end of the village at Nipe End and as you reach the eastern end of wooded Thornton Scar, turn right (5) through a gate to cross about a dozen fields by squeezer stiles to reach the main valley road (A684) by a mile post. Turn left and in about half a mile you are back in Worton.

The colourful garden of the Post Office and village store in Thornton
Left: The cliffs of Addlebrough as seen from the path across Worton Pasture

Map OS Outdoor Leisure Sheet 30, Yorkshire Dales (Northern and Central Areas)
Start/Finish Worton GR 955900
Length About 6½ miles (10.5km)
Walking time Allow 3–4 hours
Difficulty Easy field paths throughout and some lane walking

The Route in Brief

Start GR 955900, from Worton village near phone box and turn L up the lane to Cubeck.
1 Turn R then L up a steep-walled track which dies out into an almost level path across the fields, contouring around the northern slopes of Addlebrough.
2 On reaching Carpley Green Lane, turn L.
3 Just before reaching the hamlet of Carpley Green, turn L through a gate, keeping parallel to the wall on your R.
4 Cross Thornton Rust Moor to reach lane leading down to the village.
5 Turn L towards Nipe End, take the signposted path (R) near Thornton Scar to cross several fields by squeezer stiles and regain the A684 E of Worton. Turn L back to your starting point.

WENSLEYDALE · WORTON · START · River Ure
① Worton Scar · Thornton Scar · ⑤
THORNTON RUST
Worton Pasture
NORTH
② · Addlebrough · ④
Carpley Green Road · Thornton Rust Moor
Carpley Green ③
ONE MILE
1.6KM

97

PENHILL BEACON

Penhill Beacon, the Wensleydale face of Penhill, is a traditional signalling place which has been used to communicate news to the Dales since at least 1588, when it sent out a fiery warning of the approaching Spanish Armada. Although not the highest point on Penhill between Waldendale and Coverdale, Penhill Beacon is visible for many a mile, from as far away as the edge of the North York Moors across the Vale of York. The highest point of Penhill is actually the little-visited Height of Hazely (1814ft/553m), a boggy mile to the west. Penhill Edge reaches 1727ft/(526m), and the Beacon stands at 1685ft (514m) – but when you have as commanding a presence as Penhill Beacon, mere height counts for little.

The name Penhill indicates a Celtic ancestry, originating from the Welsh pen for hill or top, and as with Addlebrough higher up the dale, there are extensive Bronze Age settlements and field systems on the western edge of the hill on Burton Moor, above the village of West Burton in Waldendale.

Our walk starts from West Witton, nestling at the foot of Penhill in Wensleydale. Walk west out of the village on the Aysgarth road, turning left (**1**) opposite the former village school into a walled lane which leads onto an enclosed track known as Green Gate. This climbs up to a disused quarry (left) at Nossill End. Crossing High Lane at Stony Gate (**2**), you leave the green lane and start the ascent of the open fell towards the beckoning crags of Penhill above.

Crossing the first 'step' of Penhill (Harrow Ridge), you bear left towards the spoil heaps of the former Penhill Quarry before turning steeply up to the right (**3**) on a sunken track which leads between the crags of Black Scar and Penhill Scar and onto the plateau top.

Approaching the summit of Penhill Beacon, with Lower Wensleydale below and the Vale of York beyond

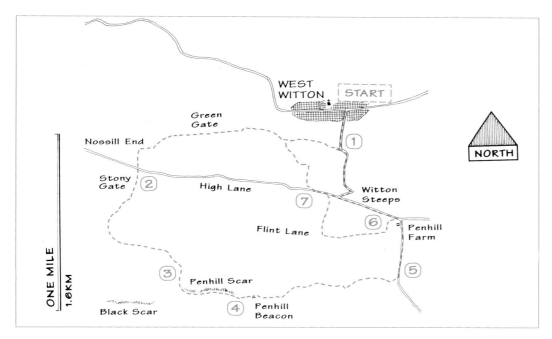

WEST WITTON | START |
Green Gate
Nossill End
Stony Gate ②
High Lane
⑦
Witton Steeps
Flint Lane
⑥
Penhill Farm
③
Penhill Scar
⑤
Black Scar
④ Penhill Beacon

①

NORTH

ONE MILE
1.6KM

FACT FILE

Map OS Outdoor Leisure Sheet 30, Yorkshire Dales (Northern and Central Areas)
Start/Finish West Witton, GR 060884
Length 6 miles (10km)
Walking time Allow 3 hours
Difficulty Green lanes and open moor, with one steep ascent

The Route in Brief

Start GR 060884, from West Witton and walk W on the Aysgarth road.
1 Opposite former school, turn L on a walled lane, and at crossroads keep straight on into Green Gate.
2 Just past former quarry at Nossill End, cross High Lane and ascend grassy track at Stony Gate towards Penhill above.
3 Bear L then turn up R to pass between Penhill Scar and Black Scar on sunken track which leads to the plateau top.
4 Turn L and walk along escarpment to Penhill Beacon.
5 Drop drown to the Melmerby–West Witton road below, and turn L to Penhill Farm.
6 Follow this lane directly down Witton Steeps to West Witton.
(**7** Alternatively, turn L along Flint Lane, and then R beyond a clump of trees to cross High Lane and meet Green Gate again to return to West Witton.)

Turn left (**4**) on the cliff-edge path north of the wall which leads up to the highest point of Penhill Scar, marked by a trig point over the wall to your right. Enjoying the views down to West Witton in the dale beneath, across to Castle Bolton under East Bolton Moor and towards Middleham to the east, you reach Penhill End and the famous Beacon.

You now have a choice of paths, all of which lead steeply but unerringly down to the West Witton–Melmerby road, where you turn left (**5**), and descend to Penhill Farm. Here you have a choice of return routes. You can (**6**) continue down this road, descending the hair-pin of Witton Steeps and go directly back to the village.

Alternatively, you can turn left at Penhill Farm (**7**) onto the pleasant walled track known as Flint Lane, turning sharply right beyond a prominent clump of trees to cross High Lane and descend onto Green Gate, retracing your route (right) back to West Witton.

A SEMER WATER ROUND

Semer Water always comes as a bit of a shock. The largest natural lake in the old North Riding sits in a glacially formed hollow in Raydale between Wether and Stake Fells, sparkling like a precious jewel in this usually lakeless land. The legend of Semer Water, how an inhospitable populace was drowned by a celestial visitor, is well-known and shared with other lakes in mountain country. Other legends include the Carlow Stone, apparently dropped by a giant at the foot of the lake, but much more likely left behind by the glacier which carved out the hollow in which the lake lies.

Our walk circles the lake in an easy afternoon stroll, taking in the two, quite different hamlets of Marsett and Stalling Busk at the lakehead, both of which have Norse origins.

Park at the large car park just south of Semer Water Bridge and walk south on the lane

This misty view of Semer Water is seen from the Carpley Green Road

towards Stalling Busk. You soon pass the Carlow Stone, a large isolated block of limestone across the lane on your left.

As the lane starts to climb, with Low Blean Farm on the left, turn right (1) across a stile on a field path which leads down towards the lake side. There are fine views here across the lake to the fields and barns on the slopes of the simply named Crag opposite.

Follow this level path through the fields eventually leaving the lake and heading up towards the ruined chapel of Stalling Busk, overlooking the lake but strangely isolated from its parent village above.

Enter Stalling Busk (the name is Norse and apparently means the stallion's bush) and turn immediately right (2) down a rough track known as Busk Lane which leads down to a ford over Cragdale Water. Cross Raydale Beck and enter Marsett alongside Marsett Beck.

At Marsett Bridge, turn right onto Marsett Lane (3) which leads easily back for just over a mile (1.6km) along the slopes of Crag, passing Carr End Farm before dropping down towards Semer Water again above its northern shore.

Where the lane starts to descend, take the stile on the right (4) which leads to a sometimes muddy path through fields and trees back to Semer Water Bridge.

Alternatively, you could stay on Marsett Lane to reach the road junction on the southern outskirts of Countersett, turning right to descend steeply to Semer Water Bridge.

Map OS Outdoor Leisure Sheet 30, Yorkshire Dales (Northern and Central Areas)
Start/Finish Car park at Semer Water Bridge GR 922876
Length About 4 miles (6.5km)
Walking time Allow 1½–2 hours
Difficulty An easy afternoon stroll

The Route in Brief

Start GR 922876, from the car park just S of Semer Water Bridge. Walk towards Stalling Busk.
1 When the lane starts to climb, take the stile (R) opposite Low Blean Farm, and follow path through fields towards the edge of the lake.

2 The path leads on into Stalling Busk. Turn R into the enclosed track of Busk Lane.
3 Cross Cragdale Water and Raydale Beck to enter Marsett, turning R at Marsett Bridge into Marsett Lane.
4 Marsett Lane is followed for just over a mile (1.6km). When it starts to descend, take the stile (R) on a path through trees to bring you back to Semer Water Bridge.

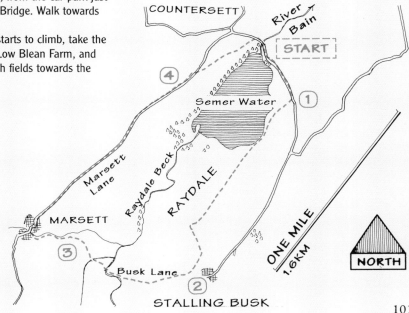

HIGH WAY TO HELL

The Moorcock Inn, an isolated but welcome hostelry, stands at 1024ft (312m), at the junction of the Kirkby Stephen and Hawes–Sedbergh roads. A landmark on the Settle–Carlisle line, it is the scene every September of an agricultural show which draws farmers from the surrounding dales on the Yorkshire–Westmorland border. It also stands on the famous Mallerstang High Road, known locally as Streets, and apparently used by Lady Anne Clifford when travelling through the Dales from Skipton in the mid-seventeenth century to visit Pendragon Castle. She records how she repaired 'these dangerous places' and 'wherein yet God was pleased to preserve me in that journey'.

The High Way passes above the isolated hamlet of Lunds. a name derived from the Norse lundr, meaning grove or copse, but there are few trees other than plantations at Lunds today. This desolate spot was famous for its remote youth hostel at Shaws (which is Old English and means the same as lund), and for its tiny church, which but for its bell-cote could be mistaken for a field barn.

Our route takes us to the dramatic ravine of Hell Gill, source of the Eden, said to have been jumped by Dick Turpin, escaping from Westmorland justice into neighbouring Yorkshire.

From the Moorcock Inn, walk down the Kirkby Stephen road and turn right onto a farm track opposite a clump of trees (1). Crossing the infant Ure, turn left on a faint path running above the river which leads to Blades Farm. Turn right here and head up through the pastures to reach the ruins of High Dyke Farm, formerly an inn frequented by highwaymen on the High Road. An adjacent cottage served as Lunds School.

Beyond the intake wall, turn left (2) and keep the wall on your left to follow that famous old highway contouring across the slopes of Lunds Fell for approximately 2 miles (3.2km). The route stands on the spring line of the fell and you pass a number of shake holes and the old farmsteads of High Way and High Hall. This is a grand promenade, and there are superb views across Mallerstang to the bold escarpment of Wild Boar Fell ahead.

Crossing stone-built Hell Gill Bridge (3), turn left down a track passing some old farmhouses and follow the tumbling beck down towards the railway line in the valley below. Just before reaching the railway bridge, a detour right will reveal the spectacular Hell Gill Force, a dashing little waterfall.

On reaching the road at Aisgill Moor Cottages (where excellent teas are now provided at the 1194ft [364m] highest point of the Settle–Carlisle railway) cross straight over and turn left (4), keeping the wall to your left to reach High Shaw Paddock. Through a gate, you cross the open fellside and contour gently right to reach the summit of Turner Hill. Despite its modest height (1521ft/ 464m), this south-eastern shoulder of Swarth Fell is a fine viewpoint for looking down the length of Wensleydale to the east, and is also a fine high-level vantage-point for train-spotters on the Settle–Carlisle.

Passing down to a gate in the wall below (5), turn left across South Lunds Pasture to cross the footbridge over the railway and down to the B6259 again. Turn right (6) and in about half a mile you are back at the Moorcock Inn.

Right: The beck starts its headlong tumble down Hell Gill Force

Map OS Outdoor Leisure Sheet 19, Howgill Fells and Upper Eden
Start/Finish Moorcock Inn GR 797927
Length 7½ miles (12km)
Walking time Allow 3–4 hours
Difficulty Serious moorland walking, for the well-equipped

The Route in Brief

Start GR 797927, from the Moorcock Inn, at the junction of the A684 Hawes–Sedbergh road with the B6259 Mallerstang route to Kirkby Stephen.
1 Walk down the Mallerstang road and take farm track opposite a clump of trees, leading R towards Yore House. Cross River Ure and turn L along river to Blades Farm.
2 Turn R uphill here through fields to ruins of High Dyke Farm. Turn L beyond intake wall onto the High Way.
3 Follow this wall and the High Way N for 2 miles (3.2km) to descend to Hell Gill Bridge. Over bridge turn L and follow gill over railway down to Aisgill Moor Cottages on B6259.
4 Cross straight over and turn L, keeping wall on your L to High Shaw Paddock.
5 Contour gently up R, across moorland to Turner Hill. Follow wall round summit to a gate (L), which leads down to footbridge over the railway.
6 Turn R at B6259, back to the Moorcock Inn.

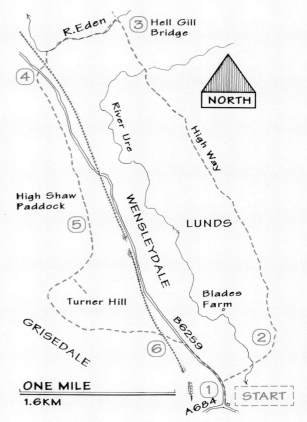

103

7

SWALEDALE:
THE WILD NORTH

Swaledale will always hold a special place in my memory for it was my introduction to the hills. A school holiday had taken us north, most of us for the first time, and as we swung off the A1 and through the time-warped feudal, castle-crowned township of Richmond, hills and moors the like of which we'd never seen before started to crowd in on either side of the winding road.

The coach turned off in the centre of the pretty stone-built village of Grinton and up an impossibly steep and narrow by-road. We were nervously glued to the windows as we wound up by the side of Grinton Gill, a dizzy precipice to our left. Eventually, our overnight stop came into view, the mock-Gothic, castellated pile of Grinton Hall Youth Hostel. We thought we were in a fairy-tale castle on top of the world.

Coming from the flatness of East Anglia, we'd never seen hills like these before and they left a lasting impression on our young minds.

Looking south to the enclosure walls on Sabron Side, near Gunnerside, central Swaledale (spot the rabbit!)

Later, when I returned to the stern northern wildness of Swaledale as an experienced Pennine bogtrotter, the hills had lost none of their majesty, perhaps only just a little of their awesomeness.

That Swaledale retains its air of rugged, northern wilderness is due as much to the vivid contrast between its flower-decked meadows and lovely villages in the dale and the bleak, watching moors above as to its geographical position. To me, the view of Muker, Thwaite or Gunnerside from the heights of the sheltering moors is the epitome of the Yorkshire Dales. It is one of the most perfect and harmonious blendings of Man with Nature to be found in these islands, with often-conflicting forces seeming to co-exist happily with never a jarring note.

Appearances, of course, can be deceptive. Up to a hundred years ago Upper Swaledale was a veritable hive of industry, as generations of farmer/miners delved deep into the moorsides in search of the precious but poisonous mineral which made Swaledale rich – galena or lead ore.

A walk up Gunnerside Gill, to the north of the attractive little village, still reveals the extensive remains of the lead industry, with many ruins still standing to show where men worked to extract the valuable blue-black ore. Unnatural platforms in the gill sides show where their waste was tipped, and many of the deep-sided green ravines which scar the hillsides around are man-made 'hushes', created when streams were dammed and then released to excavate new workings.

Whichever way you approach Swaledale, it is bound to impress. Whether you head across the Oxnop Pass from Wensleydale, down the Buttertubs from Hawes, or meet it at its head, like the Pennine Wayfarers who have trudged across Great Shunner Fell and down into Thwaite, Swaledale imposes itself on the senses.

The intricate pattern of field walls and barns, so typical of the Dales, is seen in Swaledale to perfection, with every field seeming to have its own simple little hay barn.

The clearance of the native wildwood which once carpeted Swaledale was probably started by the first slash-and-burn settlers. But the landscape we see today was to a large extent shaped by the first permanent farmers, and

The imposing keep of Richmond Castle watches over the town

their identity is easily established by a glance at the map and a study of place-names.

Of all the Yorkshire Dales, Swaledale is the home of the Norsemen. Villages like Thwaite (a clearing); Keld (a spring), Gunnerside (Gunnar's Sett) and Muker (narrow field) are all either Old Norse or Scandinavian in origin. They show that the people who named these settlements were Norsemen and Vikings who first made their way into the dale from across the Cumbrian Hills.

Even today, Swaledale is the only dale in which the surrounding hills are known locally as 'fells', the Old Norse word so common in the Lake District. Elsewhere, the hills are usually known by the Old English name of 'moors'.

The native Swaledale farmers – typically tall, thin, wiry men with an innate sense of courtesy and politeness – still have that fierce, independent spirit and love of the high, lonely places which distinguishes Norsemen from the valley-loving Anglians. And they have bred perhaps the greatest single contribution that the dale has made to the world of agriculture – the black-footed and white-nosed curly-horned Swaledale sheep. Adopted by the Yorkshire Dales National Park for its logo, the Swaledale is prized all over the uplands of Britain for its hardiness and fertility.

Ella Pontefract and Marie Hartley tell the story of the Swaledale farmer who was rather foolishly asked if he ever counted his flock of sheep. (In these days of headage payments, you should never ask a farmer exactly how many sheep he has!)

'Nay', he replied, 'I nivver count t'sheep. I ken if yan's missing. How? Why a sheep's as different as fooak; thar's nivver tweea t'seeame i' a flock.'

Pontefract and Hartley described Swaledale as 'a little country in itself'. Hemmed in by an almost continuous barrier of hills on either side, it still manages to keep itself to itself, in much the same way as its inhabitants who are descended from those original Norse settlers.

For Alfred Brown, that was the peculiar and irresistible magic of Swaledale. Climbing to the top of Ravenseat or Rogan's Seat, he said, you could look over a vast wilderness of moorlands, ridge upon ridge, stretching to seemingly limitless horizons.

It is a lonely, savage country, broken by deep clefts and wild gills, and yet in the valley of the Swale itself there are green reaches that are pure Arcady. It is a country too of secret little dales that branch out from the main valley in all directions, and whose solitude is rarely broken save by the ubiquitous sheep and the occasional shepherd who passes that way.

THE CORPSE ROAD

Keld, the last outpost of civilisation in Upper Swaledale, has been without a church, chapel or road contact with the rest of the dale for most of its 1,000 year history. So when Christianity came, the nearest church where Keld folk could be offered a Christian burial was at Grinton, 9 miles (14.5km) down the dale. And the way that the bodies were transported to Grinton was by an ancient route across the hills still known as The Corpse Road.

This easy 6 mile (10km) walk follows the Corpse Road from Keld to Muker, returning by one of the most beautiful sections of the Swale gorge. From Keld – another Norse name meaning the place of springs – take the lane back to the main road and turn left, passing Keld Lodge Youth Hostel, a former shooting lodge like Grinton's. After a few more yards, turn left down onto a rough track which crosses the Norse-sounding Skeb Skeugh by a ford.

You are now on the Corpse Road (**1**), which contours beautifully around the slopes of mighty Kisdon Hill for just over 2 miles (3.2km), before dropping down to Muker.

Walking up from Swinner Gill towards Crackpot Hall with the Swale in the background

Left: The ruined farmhouse of Crackpot Hall
Right: The pretty waterfalls of East Gill Force at East
Stonesdale above the Swale

Don't miss the charming and elegant water-fall of Arngill Force among the trees, as the first beck joins the river from the right. The track leads unerringly on, crossing West Arn Gill by a ford until the deep defile of Swinner Gill is crossed by a footbridge. There are significant lead-mining remains in Swinner Gill under Buzzard Scar above to the right.

Now the path climbs quite steeply up Bracken Hill, past the insignificant pot-hole of Aller Hole, and contours across Stony Hill. A recommended detour which can be made here is the footpath (right) which leads up to the magnificently sited ruined farmhouse of the charmingly named Crackpot Hall, which enjoys a stupendous view down the winding Swale towards Muker.

Back on the path, pass above West Wood across Beldi Hill, with its famous and very rich lead mines on the hillside above. Kisdon Force, one of the loveliest of the Swale water-falls, tumbles under Birk Hill, on the opposite bank of the river.

Crossing East Gill by another bridge, you drop down (4) to pass the beautiful cascades of East Gill Force and to the footbridge over the Swale, with Keld on the hillside opposite. It is now a short but steep step up the muddy path to the right back into Keld.

There is much of interest along the route, which passes just below a line of shake or swallow holes where the gritstone cap of Kisdon meets the limestone. The views across the valley of the Skeb Skeugh are lovely, extending to the giants at the head of the dale, including Lovely Seat, Great Shunner Fell, High Seat and Nine Standards Rigg.

After a couple of miles the track, walled now, descends past Kisdon Farm and crosses the line of the Pennine Way. There are fine views ahead, down to the silver Swale at Rampsholme Bridge. Our route joins the metalled farm access road, and zigzags down to enter the village of Muker below.

After exploring the lovely village of Muker (Norse again, meaning narrow field), retrace your steps to the lane by which you entered and cross a stile on your right (2) which leads across the fields to Rampsholme footbridge, which you saw from high on Kisdon earlier. Once across the Swale, turn left to drop down to the riverside track (3), which leads upstream along the boundary of Ivelet Wood.

Map OS Outdoor Leisure Sheet 30, Yorkshire Dales (Northern and Central Areas)
Start/Finish Keld, GR 892013
Length 6 miles (10km)
Walking time Allow 4 hours
Difficulty No steep ascents, mainly easy paths and tracks in he valley

The Route in Brief

Start GR 892013, from Keld village car park. Walk back to the main road.
1 Turn L after a few yards onto the Corpse Road, which contours S around Kisdon Hill crossing the Pennine Way near Kisdon Farm and eventually zigzagging down to Muker.
2 From Muker, take the field paths which lead to Rampsholme Bridge across the Swale.
3 Turn L onto the riverside track (Coast-to-Coast route), passing Arngill Force (R) and Swinner Gill, before rising towards Crackpot Hall (above R) and East Gill Force.
4 Descending to a footbridge over the Swale, ascend back into Keld.

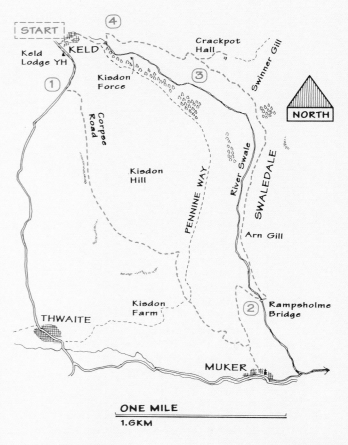

GRINTON'S INDUSTRIAL PAST

The castellated pile of Grinton Lodge Youth Hostel, on its panoramic perch overlooking Swaledale, Fremington Edge and Arkengarthdale, holds a special place in my memory. For it was here, on a school trip from my home in East Anglia, that I had my first real introduction to the hills. The Lodge was built as a shooting lodge in Victorian times and looked almost impossibly romantic as our ancient bus toiled up the long lane from Grinton village to reach it. I remember we later spent some time, in an unguarded moment, tumbling rocks into Cogden Gill far below.

Although Grinton is still surrounded by some of Yorkshire's finest grouse moors, like many Swaledale villages, it has an industrial past. This short, 4 mile (6.5km) walk, suitable for an evening stroll, takes in some of the finest remains of lead mining on the south-

Where the main valley road turns sharply by the inn, take the lane which is signposted to the youth hostel and which climbs steeply out of the village past the Manor House to the left. Passing the drive to the youth hostel on the left, keep climbing up Hirst Ridge until the lane dips down left to cross Cogden Gill by a bridge. Just over the bridge, take the track on the right (1) which ascends up the left bank of the gill. You will soon reach the remains of Grinton Smelting Mill, which operated for about 100 years from the early nineteenth century. The mill remains alongside the peat store.

Also highly conspicuous are the impressive remains of the cut-and-cover underground flue which fed air into the smelting mill from a chimney high on Sharrow Hill above. Paths lead further up the gill on either bank, or you can walk directly up through the heather

Left: The view looking towards Arkengarthdale from the summit of Sharrow Hill
Right: The castellated pile of Grinton Youth Hostel, with Fremlington Edge beyond

Looking up inside the flue on Sharrow Hill above Grinton

alongside the flue to where the chimney once stood under the crags of Sharrow Hill – a fine viewpoint (**2**).

From Sharrow Hill, descend directly on a track (**3**) to cross the Grinton–Leyburn road, and through a gate down to a walled track which ambles down to Cogden Hall. There are fine views down the dale to Marrick Priory from here. Keep to the left of Cogden Hall and farm before rejoining the B6270 valley road and turning left (**4**) back to Grinton.

112

Map OS Outdoor Leisure Sheet 30, Yorkshire Dales (Northern and Central Areas)
Start/Finish Grinton, GR 047984
Length 4 miles (6.5km)
Walking time Allow 2½ –3 hours
Difficulty Some steep climbs across moorland but nothing too serious

The Route in Brief
Start GR 047984, from the centre of Grinton village, taking the steep lane leading S to the youth hostel.
1 Pass the youth hostel on L, and where the road crosses Cogden Gill, take track (R) up L bank.
2 From the smelt mill, follow line of flue NE to the top of Sharrow Hill, across the moor.
3 Descend Cogden Moor, cross the Leyburn road and follow track to Cogden Hall.
4 Turn L to follow B6270 back to Grinton.

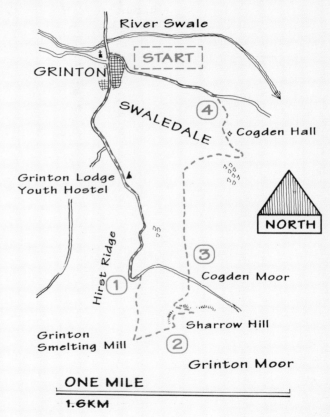

ARKENGARTHDALE: THE FORGOTTEN DALE

Although Arkengarthdale, with its strange-sounding hamlets like Whaw and Booze, is the major northern feeder dale into Swaledale, it is seldom visited. The Norse name of the dale means the valley of Arnkell's enclosure, Arnkell being a common Old Scandinavian name. Ella Pontefract records that an Arkil, son of Gospatrick, still held the estate just before the Conquest. These strange names reflect an ancient ancestry. Whaw, for example, is Old English and simply means an enclosure for cows, while Booze is thought to have obtained its amusingly alcoholic appellation from nothing more than being a house by the bow, or curve, of the Arkle Beck, which also takes its name from that early Norse settler. Sadly, there is no pub at Booze.

This easy valley walk starts and finishes at Langthwaite – another Norse name meaning the long clearing, still a perfect description of this linear hamlet. The pub at Langthwaite is known as the 'CB' after Charles Bathurst, a local landowner, and nearby is a well-preserved octagonal powder house from old CB's smelt mill.

On the edge of Scar House Woods north of Langthwaite

113

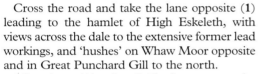

From the centre of Langthwaite, take the track up through the village, crossing fields on the edge of the woods below Booze Common to Scar House, a former shooting lodge hidden among the trees. This leads down to a stile and the road across the moors to Barnard Castle.

Cross the road and take the lane opposite (**1**) leading to the hamlet of High Eskeleth, with views across the dale to the extensive former lead workings, and 'hushes' on Whaw Moor opposite and in Great Punchard Gill to the north.

After about 1¹⁄₂ miles (2.5km), you enter the hamlet of Seal Houses, and just after a left-hand fork in the lane, take the stile on the left (**2**), descending through four fields by stiles into the hamlet of Whaw.

Turn left here and, just before the bridge, left again (**3**) to follow a farm track down to the Arkle Beck. Field paths now lead close to the tree-lined beck to a footbridge which leads back to the lane at Stang Bridge. Now follow field paths (**4**) on the western side of the beck to return back into Langthwaite near the restored parish church of St Mary's.

Right: The view looking south down Arkengarthdale from near Seal Houses

Inset: Langthwaite general stores have featured in James Herriot films

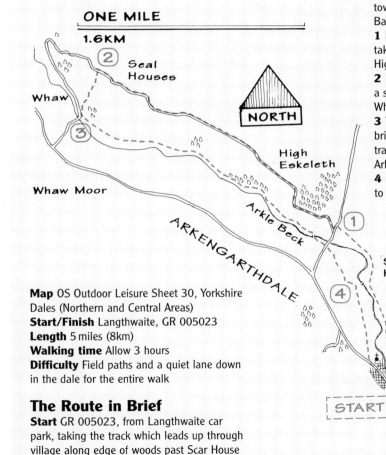

FACT FILE

ONE MILE
1.6KM

NORTH

Seal Houses

Whaw

Whaw Moor

High Eskeleth

Arkle Beck

ARKENGARTHDALE

Scar House

Booze Common

START   LANGTHWAITE

towards Stang Bridge and the Barnard Castle road.
1 From the Stang Bridge road, take the lane (opposite) through High Eskeleth to Seal Houses.
2 From Seal Houses, turn L over a stile through the fields to Whaw.
3 Turn L at the gate before the bridge in Whaw and follow tracks and field paths along Arkle Beck back to Stang Bridge.
4 Follow field paths again back to Langthwaite.

Map OS Outdoor Leisure Sheet 30, Yorkshire Dales (Northern and Central Areas)
Start/Finish Langthwaite, GR 005023
Length 5 miles (8km)
Walking time Allow 3 hours
Difficulty Field paths and a quiet lane down in the dale for the entire walk

The Route in Brief

Start GR 005023, from Langthwaite car park, taking the track which leads up through village along edge of woods past Scar House

YORKSHIRE'S YUKON

Just over a century ago Swaledale was the Yukon of the Yorkshire Dales' 'lead rush'. At the height of the industry in the 1880s, more than 4,000 miners were employed in scores of mines under these now peaceful hills. This walk from the lovely Swaledale village of Gunnerside reveals some of the best of what remains of this largely forgotten industry.

Park in the car park by the bridge in the village, and take the waymarked path which leads north up the right-hand side of Gunnerside Gill (**1**). The route soon passes a line of bunkers beside the path, used to store large pieces of lead ore. The remains of the Sir Francis level can still be seen across the gill, and the debris from two crushing mills, used to separate the ore from the rock, is also visible on either side of the stream. The rusty cast-iron cylinder lying on the opposite bank is the

Left: The view eastwards over Gunnerside Gill from the abandoned workings of Lownathwaite lead mine
Right: The view southwards over Gunnerside village, towards the slopes of Crackpot Moor

air receiver for the mine's hydraulic pump which once extracted water from the levels below.

The grassy track crosses Swina Bank to the ruins of the Bunton Mine buildings (**2**), which stand on a level shelf above the gill. Cross three shallow 'hushes' – gullies formed after streams were dammed to create a head of water which was then released to excavate the ground. The Lownathwaite Mines extending west across the gill from here are some of the earliest in the dale, first worked by Lord Philip Wharton in the mid-seventeenth century.

Continue up the narrowing valley into the heart of Gunnerside Moor to cross a clapper bridge (**3**). Now turn south below Eweleap Scar to reach the remains of the Blakethwaite Smelt Mill, where the ore was burnt to remove impurities. The prominent four-arched building is where the peat fuel taken from the moor was stored.

Climb up west (**4**) and across Lownathwaite Mea to follow another hush which leads due west past the prominent Woodward Level tip and out onto the moor. The route runs past a series of grouse butts in the heather and eventually descends by East Grain into Swinner Gill, an impressive, tree-lined gorge which contains the remains of the Beldi Mines,

Smelt Mill in Bunton Hush, a long-abandoned level in Gunnerside Gill

opened in 1771, near the junction with the Swale.

Our route then heads south on the main track (**5**) just above the intake wall; this passes above Swinner Gill and Arn Gill Wood, cross-ing West Arn Gill and above Arn Gill Scar on a high-level path. There are fine views west across the dale to Kisdon Hill beyond. The path now contours along the slopes of Black Hill on Ivelet Boards above Ivelet Wood, with views down to Muker nestling in the valley beneath and Lovely Seat to the south. It runs east round Ivelet Side and between High and Low Kisdon Scars and over Cock Crow Scar, then drops down across Kisdon Bottom to meet the road at Shore Gill (**6**) just above Gunnerside Lodge.

Walk downhill to enter Ivelet village; there is a footpath by the telephone box (**7**) signposted to Gunnerside and leading across the fields back to your starting point.

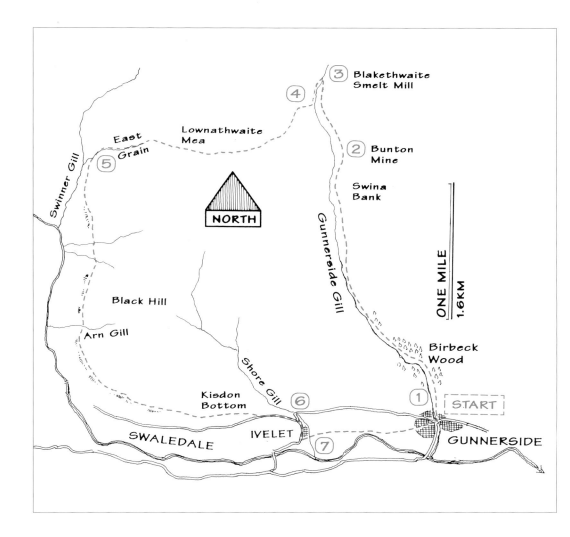

Map OS Outdoor Leisure Sheet 30, Yorkshire Dales (Northern and Central Areas)
Start/Finish Gunnerside village, GR 951982
Length About 10 miles (16km)
Walking time Allow 6 hours
Difficulty Good tracks for most of the way

The Route in Brief

Start GR 951982. From village take waymarked path to Gunnerside Gill.
1 Ascend R (E) bank of gill past remains of lead mining.
2 Cross Swina Bank to Bunton Mine. Cross three 'hushes'.
3 Ascend narrowing valley to cross clapper bridge to Blakethwaite Smelt Mill.
4 Turn S below Eweleap Scar and then W across Lownathwaite Mea for about a mile (1.6km) to descend to Swinner Gill via East Grain.
5 Turn S above gill and cross West Arn Gill to contour round Black Hill.
6 Drop down across Kisdon Bottom to meet road at Shore Gill.
7 Descend into Ivelet village and turn L by phone box across the fields back to Gunnerside.

SURRENDER TO THE OLD GANG

Just as the navvies set up their 'Tin Towns' to build the Pennine reservoirs, so 't'owd man', as the old lead miners were known, established their communities high among the hills of Swaledale. Probably the most famous of these settlements was that around the Old Gang Mines between Gunnerside Gill and Arkengarthdale. Ella Pontefract records in *Swaledale* (1934) an entry dated 1744 in Grinton's parish register of the christening of Mary Borras, born at Level House, the remains of which still stand high in Hard Level Gill. To come across these forlorn ruins high in the fells is like discovering a lost village.

It's said that the Old Gang Mines on nearby Merry Field were so rich that as much lead ore was taken from them as remains in the strange moonscape of spoil heaps left behind. Today, Nature is slowly reclaiming what was lost to industrial exploitation.

This walk from the popular picnic spot of Surrender Bridge, between Swaledale and Arkengarthdale, takes in these evocative remains on the return route from a moorland summit which just fails to reach the magic 2000ft (610m) mark, but which offers a bracing, easy walk to one of Swaledale's highest hills.

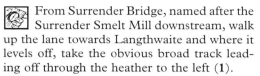 From Surrender Bridge, named after the Surrender Smelt Mill downstream, walk up the lane towards Langthwaite and where it levels off, take the obvious broad track leading off through the heather to the left (**1**).

Walk steadily up past a series of well-maintained grouse butts over Barras End. The remains of the Barras End Levels are below you to the right, the name suspiciously similar to that of the child mentioned earlier, born at Level House 250 years ago.

After about 2 miles (3.2km) of this easy moorland tramp, the going can become a bit damp as you cross the tell-tale Wetshaw Bottom. Passing a large sheepfold to your right, the flat summit of Great Pinseat, surrounded by the remains of lead mining tips on an area known just as Surrender Ground, comes into view. The actual summit is just off the path to your right and hidden behind a drystone wall (**2**). It's worth the detour, but the plateau-like summit does not offer much of a view, the best of which is looking back towards Calver Hill and Fremington Edge, down the dale the way you have come.

Returning to the bridleway, you head west through the spoil heaps to reach Forefield Rake, which follows the line of a worked-out

Left: The 'lost village' of Old Gang as approached from Surrender Bridge
Right: Surrender Bridge over the Old Gang (or Mill) Gill

Map
OS Outdoor Leisure Sheet 30, Yorkshire Dales (Northern and Central Areas)
Start/Finish Surrender Bridge, GR 989998
Length 6 miles (10km)
Walking time Allow 3 hours
Difficulty Some high moorland tracks but mostly easy walking

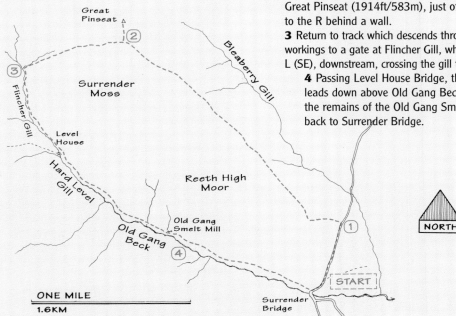

Great Pinseat

② Surrender Moss

③ Bleaberry Gill

Flincher Gill

Level House

Hard Level Gill

Reeth High Moor

Old Gang Smelt Mill

Old Gang Beck

④

① NORTH

START

Surrender Bridge

ONE MILE
1.6KM

The Route in Brief

Start GR 989998, from Surrender Bridge, on the minor road between Feetham and Langthwaite.

1 Cross bridge and walk up the lane until it starts to level off, where a broad track leads L up across the moor towards the grouse butts.

2 Follow this obvious track to the summit of Great Pinseat (1914ft/583m), just off the track to the R behind a wall.

3 Return to track which descends through old lead workings to a gate at Flincher Gill, where you turn L (SE), downstream, crossing the gill twice.

4 Passing Level House Bridge, the track leads down above Old Gang Beck through the remains of the Old Gang Smelt Mill and back to Surrender Bridge.

lead vein and leads down to Flincher Gill. Ahead are the profitable Old Gang Mines on Merry Field, a tortured moonscape of hushes, tips, rakes and shafts.

Turn left down Flincher Gill (**3**) crossing it twice by fords. It changes its name to Hard Level Gill as it reaches the remains of Level House and its bridge, where lodgings and a blacksmith's shop once existed to serve the mines.

Passing Hard Level Force you soon reach the abandoned but carefully restored remains of the Old Gang Smelt Mill, where the ore from the mines was converted from galena to the precious metal. The flue for the smelter ran half a mile up Healaugh Side to a chimney on Healaugh Crag above the mill. The furnace house, stores and blacksmith's shop are also left among a wasteland of spoil heaps. As you approach the mill near the arched entrance to the Spence Level, the massive pillars and gables of the peat store, where up to a year's supply of the locally won fuel was stored, can be seen marching across the skyline high to the left.

After a careful exploration of these fascinating remains, the track leads unmistakably back down (**4**) the northern bank of Old Gang Beck (also known as Mill Beck) to the green oasis of Surrender Bridge.

GATEWAY TO SWALEDALE

Richmond is one of the finest small market towns in England and a perfect gateway to Swaledale and the Yorkshire Dales National Park. It has some wonderful features – an ancient cobbled market-place clustered around the church of the Holy Trinity (now the Green Howards Regimental Museum), all watched over by the great Norman castle guarding the entrance to the dale from its imposing crag.

Richmond Castle is very early, originally built within twenty years of the Norman Conquest. The chief features today are the almost complete keep, built during the reign of Henry II, and Scolland's Hall.

Winding alleyways – known here as wynds – take you through more cobbled medieval streets fronted by elegant Georgian structures, such as the Royal Georgian Theatre of 1788, now restored and one of the oldest still in use in the country. To top it all, Richmond has some superb countryside within easy walking distance, including this wonderful promenade along the dramatic escarpment of Whitcliffe Scar, a pleasant precursor to the wilder country to the west.

From the Market Place, go left along Finkle Street into cobbled Newbiggin – 'new' in the late twelfth century and surely one of Richmond's most lovely streets. Turn right into Cravengate and crossing the A6108, where the road swings left, turn up into Westfields straight ahead.

Climb up this leafy avenue for about $1^{1}/_{2}$ miles (2.5km) until you leave the houses behind and the road becomes unsurfaced past Whitcliffe Farm, on your right. At High Leases Farm, on your left, turn left (**1**) through a gate to climb up through the fields to the eastern end of Whitcliffe Scar.

You can now relax and enjoy a superb promenade along this airy edge with wonderful views down into the wooded valley of the Swale below, and west into the jaws of Swaledale. After about half a mile you reach the monuments at Willance's Leap, where Robert Willance, a Richmond draper, had a miraculous escape when out hunting one foggy day in 1606. His horse fell 200ft (60m) over the cliff, but Willance suffered nothing more than a broken leg and saved himself by cutting open his dead steed and sheltering inside until help came.

Leaving this grisly reminder behind, continue along the cliff-top path (**2**) which follows a

The view from the castle across Richmond towards Swaledale

On the escarpment of Whitcliffe Scar, west of Richmond

wall round into wooded Deep Dale ahead. On reaching the Marske–Richmond road, drop down to join a farm track leading steeply down into the dry valley of Deep Dale (**3**). With rocky tors rising to your left and woods on your right,

Deep Dale has been accurately compared with the Peakland dale of the same name.

Following the signs around the farm of Low Applegarth, you cross several fields to join the path (**4**) which runs along the northern bank of the Swale and is followed through the woods to Lownethwaite Farm. Go round the farm (**5**) and follow the enclosed path to cross the

A6108, and then descend through the trees to the riverbank and over a footbridge.

Now turn left on the opposite bank (**6**) to follow either the riverside path or that through the lovely Hudswell Woods to Richmond Bridge, with its beautiful backdrop of the castle. Turn left across the bridge and it is now a short step up the hill and back into Richmond.

Map OS Pathfinder 609, Richmond and Leyburn
Start/Finish Richmond, GR 168011
Length 7½ miles (12km)
Walking time Allow 4 hours
Difficulty After a steep climb, easy cliff-top paths and through woodland and riverside pastures

The Route in Brief

Start GR 168011, from Richmond town centre, following Finkle Street, into Newbiggin and Cravengate to cross A6108 and into Westfields Lane.

1 Pass Whitcliffe Farm (R) after about 1½ miles (2.5km), then turn L at High Leases Farm to climb to Whitcliffe Scar.

2 Follow the obvious path along the top of the scar above the trees to the monuments at Willance's Leap. Keeping the wall on your R, follow the level path round into Deep Dale.

3 At the junction with the Marske–Richmond road, drop down onto a farm road leading steeply down into the dale.

4 At Low Applegarth, turn L and follow signs W of farm to join the riverside path.

5 Emerge through a wood at Lownethwaite, keeping L of the buildings to join the A6108 for a few yards.

6 Turn R through trees across a footbridge, turning L to take either the riverside or woodland path back to Richmond Bridge.

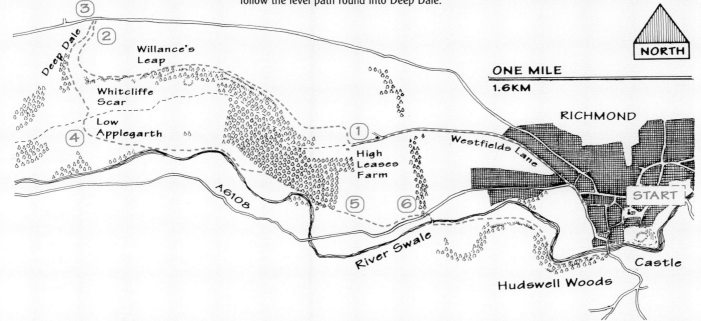

BIBLIOGRAPHY

Abbot, Stan and Whitehouse, Alan. *The Line that Refused to Die* (Leading Edge, 1990)

Allen, Bob. *Escape to the Dales* (Michael Joseph, 1992)

Boyd, Donald. *On Foot in Yorkshire* (Maclehose, 1932)

Boyd, Donald and Monkhouse, Patrick. *Walking in the Pennines* (Maclehose, 1937)

Brown, A.J. *Four Boon Fellows* (Country Life, 1928)

—— *Moorland Tramping in West Yorkshire* (Country Life, 1931)

—— *Striding through Yorkshire* (Country Life, 1938)

—— *Broad Acres* (Country Life, 1948)

Brumhead, Derek. *Geology Explained in the Yorkshire Dales and on the Yorkshire Coast* (David & Charles, 1979)

Forder, John and Eliza and Raistrick, Arthur. *Open Fell Hidden Dale* (Frank Peters, 1985)

Forder, John and Eliza. *Hill Shepherd* (Frank Peters, 1989)

—— *Life in the Hills* (Frank Peters, 1991)

Ford, Trevor. *Ingleborough Cavern and Gaping Gill* (np, 1979)

Hannon, Paul. *Walks in Nidderdale* (Hillside, 1985)

—— *80 Dales Walks* (Cordee, 1989)

—— *Freedom of the Dales* (Hillside, 1992)

Harding, Mike. *Walking the Dales* (Michael Joseph, 1986)

Hartley, Marie and Ingilby, Joan. *The Wonders of Yorkshire* (Dent, 1959)

Joy, David (ed). *The Dalesman – a Celebration of 50 Years* (Pelham, 1989)

Lund, Geoff; Muir, Richard and Colbeck, Maurice. *Yorkshire Dales Stonewaller* (Dalesman, 1992)

Marsh, Terry. *The Pennine Mountains* (Hodder & Stoughton, 1989)

—— *Fifty Classic Walks in the Pennines* (Sigma, 1994)

Mitchell, W.R. *Wild Pennines* (Hale, 1976)

Mitchell, W.R. and Joy, David. *Settle to Carlisle* (Dalesman, 1987)

Muir, Richard. *The Dales of Yorkshire* (Macmillan, 1991)

Norway, Arthur H. *Highways and Byways in Yorkshire* (Macmillan, 1911)

O'Riordan, Timothy; Wood, Christopher, and Shadrake, Ann. *Landscapes for Tomorrow* (Yorkshire Dales National Park, 1992)

Palmer, William T. *Odd Corners in the Yorkshire Dales* (Skeffington, 1937)

Phillips, Guy Ragland. *Brigantia* (Routledge & Keegan Paul, 1976)

Pontefract, Ella and Hartley, Marie. *Swaledale* (Dent, 1934)

—— *Wensleydale* (Dent, 1936)

—— *Wharfedale* (Dent, 1938)

Poucher, W.A. *The Backbone of England* (Country Life, 1946)

—— *The Peak and Pennines* (Constable, 1966)

Priestley, J.B. *English Journey* (Heinemann, 1934)

Raistrick, Arthur. *Green Tracks on the Pennines* (Dalesman, 1965)

—— *The Pennine Dales* (Eyre Methuen, 1968)

—— *The West Riding of Yorkshire* (Hodder & Stoughton, 1970)

—— *Prehistoric Yorkshire* (Dalesman, 1976)

—— *Vikings, Angles and Danes in Yorkshire* (Dalesman, 1976)

—— *Monks and Shepherds in the Yorkshire Dales* (Yorkshire Dales National Park, 1976)

—— *The Romans in Yorkshire* (Dalesman, 1977)

—— *Ice Age in Yorkshire* (Dalesman, 1978)

—— *The Pennine Walls* (Dalesman, 1978)

—— *Malham and Malham Moor* (Dalesman, 1983)

—— *The Lead Industry of Wensleydale and Swaledale. Vol. 1, The Mines* (Moorland, 1991)

Ree, Harry and Forbes, Caroline. *The Three Peaks of Yorkshire* (Wildwood House, 1983)

Riley, W. *The Yorkshire Pennines of the North-West* (Jenkins, 1934)

Sellers, Gladys. *The Yorkshire Dales, a Walker's Guide* (Cicerone, 1984)

Simmons, I.G. (ed) *Yorkshire Dales National Park* (HMSO, 1971)

Smith, Roland. *Wildest Britain* (Blandford, 1983)

—— *Walking the Great Views* (David & Charles, 1991)

—— *On Foot in the Pennines* (David & Charles, 1994)

Speakman, Colin. *A Yorkshire Dales Anthology* (Hale, 1981)

—— *Portrait of North Yorkshire* (Hale, 1986)

—— *The Dales Way* (Dalesman, 1987)

Speakman, Colin and Morrison, John. *Settle–Carlisle Country* (Leading Edge, 1990)

Sutcliffe, Halliwell. *The Striding Dales* (Warne, 1929)

Tobin, Bob and Keis, Lizzie. *Trailside Flowers* (Yorkshire Dales National Park, 1993)

Unsworth, Walt. *The Pennine Playground* (Penguin, 1984)

—— *Classic Walks in the Yorkshire Dales* (Oxford Illustrated Press, 1989)

Wainwright, A. *Pennine Way Companion* (Westmorland Gazette, 1968)

—— *Walks in Limestone Country* (Westmorland Gazette, 1970)

—— *Walks on the Howgill Fells* (Westmorland Gazette, 1972)

Wainwright, A. and Geldard, Ed. *Wainwright in the Limestone Dales* (Michael Joseph, 1991)

Waltham, Tony. *Yorkshire Dales: limestone country* (Constable, 1987)

—— *Yorkshire Dales National Park* (Webb & Bower/Michael Joseph, 1987)

Wright, Geoffrey N. *Roads and Trackways of the Yorkshire Dales* (Moorland, 1985)

—— *The Yorkshire Dales* (David & Charles, 1986)

INDEX

Page numbers in *italics* indicate illustrations

Abbey, Bolton, 13, *15*, 16, 43; Fountains, 10, 13, 33, 39–41, *39–40*, 43, 49; Jervaulx, 10, 89
Addleborough, 8, 9, 95–7, *95–6*
Airedale, 45, *45*
Airton, 52–3
Aislabie, William, 41
Amerdale Dub, 22
Apedale, 89
Appletreewick, 15, 16, 19
Arant Haw, 75
Arkengarthdale, 6, *110*, 111, 113–15, *114–15*, 120
Arn Gill Wood, 118
Askrigg, *86*, 87
Attermire, 55, 60–2, *60–1*
Auden, W. H., 7, 8
Austwick, 55, 65, 67
Authulf, 95
Aysgarth Falls, 87, 89–92, *90*

Bainbridge, 26, 87, 95
Barbondale, 77
Barden Tower, 13, 15
barns, *10*, *12*, 4, 47, *53*, 101, 105; Crookacre, 22
Barras End, 122
Bathurst, Charles, 113
Beckermonds, 13, 26
Beck, Alum Pot, 68, *68*; Arkle, 113, 114; Austwick, 67; Barben, 19; Beldon, 92; Cam Gill, 27; Chapel, 57, 75; Clapham, 67, 70, 71; Cautley Holme, 82, 83; Dib, 21, 22; Dowber Gill, 28; Fell, 34, 35, 71; Fir, 19; Force Gill, 83; Gordale, 44, 49, 51; Great Agill, 16; Green Field, 13; Hebden,

24, *25*; How Stean, 33; Hull Pot, 59; Joy, 19; Kirkby, 52; Malham, 45, 46; Marsett, 101; Old Gang, 122; Oughtershaw, 11; Raydale, 101; Sell Gill, 68; Skyreholme, 19; Straw, 4
Beecroft, *54*
Bewerley, 31
Bigland, John, 55
Bishopsdale, 9, 87, 89
Blackfell Top, *28*
Blake, William, 82
Booze, 113
Bouthwaite, 33
Brackenbottom, 58
Bram Rigg Top, 75, 83
Brimham Rocks, *30*, 31, 34–5, *34*
Brown, Alfred J., 4, 10, 31, 87, 106, 128
Buckden, 26; Bridge, 27; Pike, 14, 16, 26–7, *26*; Rake, 26
Burges, William, 40
Burnsall, 15, 19–20
Butter Haw, 15

Calders, 83
Calf, The, 75, 82, 83
Cam Houses, 11
Camden, William, 15
Carperby, 90, 92
Carpley Green, 9, 95
Castle Bolton, 89–91, 99
Castle Dykes henge, 8
Castle, 10; Bolton, 89–91, *91*; Middleham, 10, 89; Richmond, 10, *106*, 123; Skipton, 10
Cautley, 82–3; Crag, *74*, 75, 82, 83; Spout, 75, 82–3, *82*

Caves, 8, 31, 47, 55, 60–2, 68–9; Albert, 62; Attermire, 60–2, *60–1*; Austwick Beck Head, 67; Birkwith, 68; Blackpot, 62; Clapham Beck, 71; Diccan, 68; Douk Ghyll, 58; Foxholes, 8; Ingleborough, 8, 55, 71; Jubilee, 55, 62; Stump Cross, 8; Victoria, 8, 55, *61*, 62; Wet, 62; White Scar, 8, 55
Cawden, *44*
Chapel-le-Dale, 57
Clapdale, 8, 55, 70–1; Drive, 70
Clapham, 8, 70–3; Bottom, 71
Cogden Hall, 112
Conistone, 14, 21, 22; Bridge, 22; Pie, 21
Coonthard Brow, 83
Countersett, 101
Coverdale, 29, 86, 98
Covill, 33
Crackpot Hall, *107–8*, 108
Crag, 101
Cragdale Water, 101
Craven limestone, 7, 21–3, 43–73; Mid-fault, 43–5, 47; North fault, 44
Crummackdale, 65–7, *66*
Cubeck, 95

Deep Dale, 124
Deepdale, 6, *53*, 77
Dent, 75, 77, *77*, 80, *81*; fault, 77, 80; station, 78, *78*
Dentdale, 6, 11, 74–83, *76*
Dib Side, 19
Dike, Black, 28; Tor, 28–9
Dodderham Moss, 78

Dowber Gill Wham, 28
Druids, 31, 34–5; Idol, 34

East Stonesdale, *108*
Edge Top, 25
Edge, Dale, 37; Fremington, 111, *111*, 121; Hoober, 47; Penhill, 98; Thrope, 37
Elbolton, *14*, 15

Farrer, Reginald, 70, 71
Fell Beck, 35
Fell, 106; Barden, 8, 15, 16; Baugh, 82; Birks, 26; Carle, 36; Crag, *86*; Dodd, 93; Firbank, 77; Fountains, 16, 58; Great Knoutberry, 75, 78; Great Shunner, 6, 94, 105, 108; Howgill, 7, 11, *72–3*, 75, 77, 80, 82–3; Kirkby, 47; Lunds, 102; Mickle, 57; Middleton, 80; Simon, *57*; Stake, 100; Swarth, 85, 102, Pike, 85; Wether, *86*, 93, 100; Wild Boar, 84–5, *85*, 88, 102
Forefield Rake, 121
Foster, Willie, 13
Fox, George, 77
Freeholders Wood, 90–2 *passim*

Galloway Gate, 78
Gargrave, 11
Garsdale, 75–7, 93; station, 79
Gawthrop, 80
Geology, 6–8, 13, 14, 44, 49, 55, 57, 65, 75, 87; Yoredale series, 8, 55, 75
Gill Heads, 19
Gill, Ais, 84, *84*; Arten, 78;

Birkwith, 68; Bolton, 24; Cogden, 111; East, 108; Far Cote, 85; Flincher (Hard Level), 122; Flinter, *76*, 80; Fossdale, 89, 94; Great Punchard, 114; Grinton, 105; Gunnerside, 105, *116*, 117, *118*, 120; Halton, 59; Hebden, 24; Hell, 102; Intake, 37; Lover, 93; Old Gang, *121*; Oliver, 80; Pen-y-Ghent, 58; Pickering, 83; Posforth, 16; Shivery, 93; Shore, 118; Swere, 83; Swinner, *107*, 108, 117, 118; Trollers, 16, *18*, 19–20; Trow, 55, *70*, 71; Twizling, 36, 37; West Arn, 108; Woo, 36
Glasshouses, 31
Gordale, 44, *44*, 49–51
Gragareth, 78
Grass Wood nature reserve, 21
Grassington, 4, 9, 14, 21–3
Gray, Thomas, 44, 49
Great Agill Bottom/Head, 16
Great Coum, 77, 80
Great Dummacks, 83
Great Pinseat, 121
Greenber, 91
Grinton, 105, 107, 111–12; Smelting Mill, 111, *112*; Youth Hostel, 105, 111, *111*
Grizedales, 47
Gunnerside, 10, 56, 117, *117*

Hanlith, 51, 53
Hannon, Paul, 128
Harber Scar Lane, 68
Harding, Mike, 75
Hardraw, 89, 94; Force, 87, 89, 93, *93*, 94

Hartley, Marie, 13, 106, 128
Hartlington Hall, 19
Hawes, 4, 87, 89, 93–4
Healaugh Crag, 122; Side, 122
Hebden, 24–5
Height of Hazely, 98
High Bishopside, *32–3*
High Clint, 93
High Dene, 25
High Eskeleth, 114
High Seat, 108
High Shaw, 94, 102
Hill forts, 9–10, 57, 71, 95
Hill, Beldi, 108; Birk, 108; Bracken, 108; Calver, 121; Crag, 80; Dead Man's, 33, 36; Dean Moor, 46; Great Close, 47; Helmsike, 78; Kail, 19; Kisdon, 4, *107–8*, 118; Pendle, 16; Pike, 93–4; Pikedaw, 47–8; Plover, 55; Rye Loaf, 47; Seaty, 51; Sharrow, 111–12; Shorkley, 45; Stony, 108; Tan, 11; Turner, 102, Warber, 52; Wassa, 2
History, 8–10, 43, 55, 57, 71, 95, 98
Hole Bottom, 24, *25*
Horton-in-Ribblesdale, 55, 58–9, 68–9
How Stean Gorge, 36
Hubberholme, 13, 26
'hushes', 105, 114, 117

Ingilby, Joan, 128
Ingleborough, 7–11 *passim*, 26, 55, 57, *57*, 63, *64*, 70–3, 75, 78, 93 *see also* Caves
Ingleton, 8, 57, 63–4; Glens, 7, 63

Ivelet, 118; Wood, 108

Kail, *14*, 15, 19
Keld, 106–8
Kettlewell, 21–3, *22*, 28–9
Kilnsey, 14, 21, 43; Crag, 8, 13–14, 21, *21*
Kingsdale, 77
Kingsley, Charles, 44, 87
Kirkby Lonsdale, 77
Kirkby Malham, 52–3, *52*
Kirkby Stephen, 84, 102
Kisdon Bottom, 118
Knoll Top, 35
Knox Manor, 35

Langstrothdale, 6, 8, *12*, 13, 26, 59; Chase, 13, 26
Langthwaite, 113–14, *114*
Lea Green, 14, 21, 22; Yeat, 78
Little Hunters Sleets, 29
Littondale, 6, 14, 22
Lofthouse, 33
Long Crag, 28
Lord's Seat, 16
Lovely Seat, 6, 93, 94, 108, 118
Lover Gill Head, 93
Low Clint, 93
Low Haygarth Farm, *74*, 82
Low Laithe, 34, 35
Lownathwaite Mea, 117
Lul Beck, 33

Malham, 4, 9, 43–6, 49, 51, 52; Cove, 7, 8, 43–6; Tarn, *42*, 43–6, *47*, House, *42*, 44, 46
Malhamdale, 42–53, *45*, *47*
Mallerstang, 84–5; High Road, 102
Marrick Priory, 112
Marsett, 100, 101
Mastiles, 51; Lane, 13, 49–51, *50*
Meugher, 33, 37
Middleham, 10, 89, 99
Middlesmoor, 33, 36–8, *37*

Mill Beck, 80
Mill Scar Lash, 14
Mining, calamine, 47, 48; lead, 10, 14, 24, 28, 35, 37, 105, 108, 111, 114, *116*, 117–22
Moorcock Inn, 84, 102–3
Moorland, 8, 14, 15, 31, 33, 55, 71, 105, 114
Moor, Bewerley, 33; Borrins, 68; Dean, 46; East Bolton, 99; Fountains Earth, 33, 36; Foxup, 59; Grassington, 14; Gunnerside, 117; Hanlith, 51; Horton, 59; In, 36; Malham, 43, 47; Masham, 26; Mastiles, 7; Mossy, 25; Nidderdale, 26; Stean, 37; Thornton Rust, 97; West Burton, 98; Whaw, 114; Woogill, 36
Moughton, 8, 55, 67
Muir, Dr Richard, 31
Muker, 4, 105–8, 118

Nab, The, 84
Nappa Cross, 47–8
New Close, 21, 51; Knotts, 49
Newby Cote, 71; Moss, 71
Nidderdale, 13, 28, 30–41
Nine Standards Rigg, 108
Norber, *9*, 55, 65–7; Brow, 67; erratics, 65–7, *66*
Norsemen, 10, 13, 77, 106
Nossil End, 99

'Ocky', The, 77, 80–1, *80*
Old Gang, 120–2, *120*; Smelt Mill, 122
Oughtershaw, 26

Parcevall Hall, 19
Pass, Buttertubs, 93, 94, 105; Oxnop, 105
Pasture, 13, 21, 22, 43; Appletreewick, 19; Cam, 29;

Dib, 21; High, 68; High Ox, 21; Laund Plantation, 16; South Lunds, 102; Worton, 95
Pateley Bridge, 8, 31, 33, 39
Penhill Beacon, 8, 98–9, *98*
Pennant, Thomas, 15
Pen-y-Ghent, 8, 11, 26, 55, 57–9, *58*, 67
Plants, lime-loving, 8, 21
Pontefract, Ella, 13, 24, 106, 113, 120, 128
Posforth Bridge, 16
pot-hole, 8, 19, 28, 31, 33, 55, 68–9, 71, 90; Aller Hole, 108; Alum, 8, 68, *68;* Angerholme, 84; Bar, 71; Gaping Gill, 8, 55, 68, 71, *71*; Goyden, 33, 37; Hell Hole, 19; Hull, 8, 55, 59; Hunt, 55; Long Churn, 68; Manchester Hole, 37; Providence, 28; Sell Gill Holes, 68; swallow, 78, 97; Thack, 71
Priestley, J. B., 4
Prior Rakes, 46

Rain Stang, 36
Raistrick, Arthur, 7, 8, 43, 44, 57, 77, 128
Rakes Wood, 26
Rampsholme Bridge, 108
Ramsgill, 33
Raven Ray, 63
Ravenseat (Rogan's Seat), 106
Raydale, 87, 100
Reservoir, 31, 33, 36; Angram, 28, 33, 36, 37; Gouthwaite, 33, 36, 37; Mossy Moor, *24*, 25; Scar House, 28, 33, 36, *36*, 37
Ribblehead, 11, 55, 57
Ribblesdale, *7*, 9, 54–73
Richmond, 11, 105, 123–5, *123*
Rigodunum, 57, 71
Ripley, 31

River, Aire, 4, 44, 46, 52, 53, Head, 44, 46; Dee, 75, 78; Doe, 57, 63; Eden, 83, 102; Lune, 75; Nidd, 31, 33; Ouse, 4; Rawthey, 82, 83; Ribble, 11, 59; Skeb Skeugh, 107–8; Skell, 40–1; Skirfare, 14, 22; Swale, 4, 5, 124; Twiss, 57, 63–4; Ure, 8, 90, 93, 102; Wharfe, 4, 11, 15, 16, *17*, 27, 59
Rooke, Major Hayman, 31
Ruskin, John, 15, 90

Sabron Side, *104*
Sand Tarn, 84
Scar House, 114; Woods, *113*
Scar, 47, 55; Arn Gill, 118; Attermire, 55, 62; Black, 24, 98; Blackbed, 84; Brackenbottom, 58; Buzzard, 108; Care, 25; Cock Crow, 118; Combe (Dent), 80; Ewe Close, 19; Eweleap, 87; Gordale, 8, 43, 44, 47, 49, *49*; Great, 7, 45; Knipe, 22; Kisdon, 6, 118; Long, 66, 67; Penhill, 98– 9; Robin Proctor's, 65, *65*; Sheep, 68; Southerscales, 8; Swineber, 22; Thornton, 97; Thwaite, 67; Twistleton, 63; White Stone, *66*; Whitecliffe, 123, *124*
Scosthrop, 52
Scott, Sir Walter, 16
Seal Houses, 114
Sedbergh, 7, 75
Sedbusk, 93
Sedgwick, Adam, 77
Semer Water, 87, 95, 100–1, *100*
Settle, 8, 11, 47, 57, 60, 62; –Carlisle railway, 11, 55, 57, 68, 78, 84, *84*, 102
Silverdale, 58
Simon's Seat, 15, *15*, 16, 19

Skelldale, 10, 33, 41
Skyreholme, *10*, *15*, 16, 19; Dam, 19
Smelthouses, 31, 35
Stalling Busk, 100–1
Starbotton, 6, 13, 27, *27*
Stone, 23; Carlow, 87, 100, 101; Devil's, 95; Hen, 16; Mermaid, 87; Thwaite, 6; Yockenthwaite, 8
Stony Raise, 95
Strid, The, 15–17; Wood, 16
Studley Royal, 33, 39–41, *40*
Sulber Gate, 67; Nick, *7*, 68
Summerbridge, 31
Surrender Bridge, 120–2, *121*; Ground, 121; Smelt Mill, 121
Swaledale, 4, 10, 11, 104–23, *104*, *107*
Swilla Glen, 63
Swina Bank, 117
Sypeland Crags, 36

Tennyson, Lord, 15
Thieves Moss, 67
Thornton, *97*; Force, 7, 57, 63, *63*
Thorpe, 15
Thwaite, 105, 106
Tor Mere Top, 27, 29
Trougate, 46
Truckle Crags, 16
Turner, J. M. W., 15
Turpin, Dick, 102
Twistleton, 55; Glen, 64

Underbank, 80

Valley of Desolation, 16
Viaduct, 63; Ais Gill, 84; Artengill, 78, *79*; Batty Moss, 55, *56*

Wainwright, A., 11, 70, 82, 84
Waldendale, 26–7, 87, 98
Walker, Adam, 49
Ward, James, 49

Warrendale Knots, 60, 62
Wassa Bank, 22
Water Sinks, 46
Waterfall, 7, 28, 44, 49, 57, 63–4, 82–3, 87, 94; Arngill, 108; Beezley, 63–4; Black Force, 75; Black Scar, 24; Cat's Leap, 63–4; East Gill, *109*; Gordale, 44, 49; Hard Level, 122; Hell Gill, 102, *103*; Holly Bush Spout, 63; Janet's Foss, 44, 49; Kisdon, 108; Pecca, 63; Posforth, 16; Snow, 63–4, Spout, 75 *see also individual headings*
Watlowes, 44–6
Way, Coast-to-Coast, 11; Cycle, 71; Dales, 11, 16, 19, 21, 27, 78; High, 102; Nidderdale, 31, 36; Pennine, 11, 46, 53, 57–9, 94, 108; Ribble, 11; Three Peaks, 11, 28, 55–7, 59, 68
Wedber Wood, 49
Weets Top, 51
Wensleydale, 9, 10, 11, 86–103
Wesley, Charles, 87
West Burton, 87
West Witton, 98–9; Steeps, 99
Wetshaw Bottom, 121
Wharfedale, 6, 7, 8, 11, 13–29
Whaw, 113, 114
Whernside, 14, 16, 28–9, *28*, 33, 37, 55, 57, *72–3*, 75, 77, 78, 93
Widdale, 87, 93
Willance's Leap, 123
Winder. The, 75
Windy Pike, 51
Woodale, 33
Wordsworth, William, 15, 43, 44
Worton. *89*, 95, 97

Yarlside, 83
Yarnbury, 14
Yockenthwaite, 8, 13, 26